C000046849

CHANGING BEHAVIOUR

Teaching Children with Emotional and Behavioural Difficulties in Primary and Secondary Classrooms

CHANGING BEHAVIOUR

Teaching Children with Emotional and Behavioural Difficulties in Primary and Secondary Classrooms

SYLVIA MCNAMARA
GILL MORETON

David Fulton Publishers
London

David Fulton Publishers Ltd
2 Barbon Close, London WC1N 3JX

First published in Great Britain by
David Fulton Publishers 1995
Reprinted 1996

Note: The right of Sylvia McNamara and Gill Moreton to be identified as the authors of this work has been asserted by them in accordance with the Copyright, Designs and Patents Act 1988.

Copyright © Sylvia McNamara and Gill Moreton

British Library Cataloguing in Publication Data

A catalogue record for this book is available from the British Library

ISBN 1-85346-350-7

All rights reserved. No part of this publication may be reproduced, stored in a retrieval system or transmitted, in any form, or by any means, electronic, mechanical, photocopying, recording or otherwise, without the prior permission of the publishers.

Designed by Almac Ltd., London
Typeset by Harrington & Co
Printed in Great Britain by Bell & Bain Ltd., Glasgow

Contents

Introduction

This book addresses the issue of the effective teaching, learning and inclusion of those pupils who are usually viewed as having Emotional and Behavioural Difficulties. The authors of this book take the view that Emotional and Behavioural Difficulties have two aspects: the feelings, motivations, expectations and behaviours of the teacher and also those of the child.

This book is about addressing both aspects within the framework of the National Curriculum. The reason for this is that in our experience, anything that is not placed in a curriculum framework is perceived by the teachers as creating additional work for them in an already overcrowded timetable, and by the students as being not relevant to 'real school work', which is assessed by the examination and testing system. Some of the exercises in this book may be recognised by teachers of Personal and Social Education but this book seeks to embed the structures into the assessed curriculum framework, helping to overcome students' perceptions that they are not important. To that extent the strategies and structures suggested in this book represent a whole teaching methodology.

Our own experience shows that by using the structures suggested to deliver the curriculum, teachers will find that in the long term they save time, because they are no longer dealing with petty disputes and therefore they can deliver the curriculum more effectively to all their pupils. In addition they will be able to start to meet the needs of pupils with emotional and behavioural difficulties.

The problem that such pupils pose for teachers is that they arouse powerful feelings of confusion and frustration. Teachers have reported to us their sense of failure and inadequacy – it is as if their competence as a teacher is being assessed, by both managers and parents, on their ability to deal with students who cause disruptions in the class. The authors take the view that if teachers have not been shown a set of alternative strategies for dealing with both the behaviour of the pupils and the feelings aroused in themselves then they only have the experience of how they themselves were treated at school. This book seeks to provide teachers with alternative strategies so that they can not only maintain control but maintain it in a different way.

It is our belief that all children respond to the environment that they are in and that children with emotional and behavioural difficulties are no exception. This environment consists of:

- teachers and their behaviour;
- rules – both openly stated and in the hidden curriculum;
- peers and their behaviour.

This book recommends that when seeking to change disruptive behaviour, instead of initially focusing on the particular pupil, teachers first look at teacher behaviour and language, appropriate rules and their formation in the classroom and the skills and behaviour demonstrated by the pupil's peers.

There is an understandable tendency for teachers and special needs co-ordinators to focus on the particular pupil. Indeed the 1981 Education Act and the 1993 Act with the 1994 *Code of Practice* and 1994 *Pupils with Problems* (D.F.E.), outline the numbers of different professionals who contribute to providing information to assist in the identification of pupils who have special needs, including those who have Emotional and Behavioural difficulties. These professionals include educational psychologists, social workers, teachers, medical personnel and health workers, and parents. Although this helps to build up a more complete picture of the child, many of the problems are ones over which the classroom teacher has no control. For example, poverty, race, past sexual abuse might be factors which are influencing a child's behaviour. We believe that because the pupil has problems other than those experienced in the classroom, many find that they are unable to respond to focused attempts to help them function in school. Whilst we recognise such pupils need attention from other professionals, our experience shows that when teachers change their focus and concentrate their main efforts on changing the classroom environment, which we know also exerts a powerful influence on the pupil, then their efforts with the pupil become more effective. Additionally, teachers start to feel more powerful and therefore less frustrated. This seems to be because they are focusing on the things over which they have control rather than the things over which they have very little.

A useful way of looking at disruptive behaviour is to see the behaviour as, to a certain extent, a manifestation of a group feeling, being acted out on behalf of the rest of the group. Indeed, the American terminology for disruptive pupils is 'acting out'. It is our belief that the feelings that are on display when a child 'erupts' are to some extent the feelings of all the pupils. Boredom, a sense of injustice, fear of failure or being shown up, frustration or hurt are shared by all. Other pupils bottle up these feelings, until break times, when they spill out and are identified as bullying behaviour, vandalism, withdrawal and isolation. In chapter three we explain the role of the peer group in this.

Being in school is to do with not being an individual but being part of many groups. Pupils who behave in a way that causes disruption are often those who are striving for recognition as individuals, or as it is often called, attention seeking.

It seems to us that it is understandable that pupils have strong feelings aroused in the classroom because it isn't easy to:

- be in a class of thirty others of the same age;
- feel a sense of achievement in all areas of the curriculum;
- manage being in a timetable;
- be in an institution with many complex rules and norms;
- relate to an adult in a position of authority;
- cope with large numbers of other youngsters throughout the breaks.

We share the view that there is a continuum of behaviour that is being manifested by different pupils all the time and it depends on where the teacher or the school draws the line as to what is deemed to be unacceptable. When a pupil strays over that threshold then they are labelled 'Emotionally and Behaviourally Disturbed'.

In order to bring evidence, systems, order and therefore fairness to an area rife with powerful feelings, we have found elements of the behaviourist approach to be useful in training teachers and pupils alike to seek out and describe actual behaviours as evidence. The book outlines clearly which aspects are helpful and how to teach these skills to pupils. However, the book also outlines a different approach which draws on a number of different psychological theories including: counselling, self-esteem, transactional analysis, attribution and personal responsibility. These are discussed in detail in chapters one, two and three and are then used throughout the book as a foundation for restructuring the classroom.

The reasons for presenting the psychological foundations are twofold. One is to present an argument that is persuasive enough to convince teachers that this approach is worth trying, the other is so that teachers who do start to use the strategies presented have a clear idea about why they are doing what they are doing and how the pupil might be expected to respond. This way of working takes time, it does not represent a 'quick fix' to disruption, it is a new way of working for both the pupil and the teacher and both will initially find this difficult. The pay off for both in the long term is the independence gained by all concerned and a drop in stress levels for teachers. The skill of the teacher, however, will be required to adapt the strategies for their own specialist subject and age group of pupils. In our experience this is possible if teachers understand the theoretical foundations behind the exercise.

This book builds on previous recommendations (Elton Report, D.E.S. 1989) for positive classroom ethos and management as a way of addressing discipline issues and extends them to include pupils with emotional and behavioural difficulties. It explores in detail both the skills for teachers and the skills for pupils needed to achieve a positive classroom ethos and answers the question of how these skills can be taught to pupils.

CHAPTER 1

Antecedents of Emotional and Behavioural Difficulties

Rationale

The premise of this book is that emotional and behavioural difficulties are to do with pupils who are so badly hurt and in so much pain that they are angry. It is our belief that they express their anger in a place that is safe: to that extent, expression of anger in school could be seen as positive. This pain might be brought in from home or it might be caused by or at school. It seems to us that the reason why dealing with this angry behaviour is so difficult for teachers is because they too feel the pupil's pain. In effect then, emotional and behavioural difficulties are to do with children who are hurting but don't know what to do with that pain.

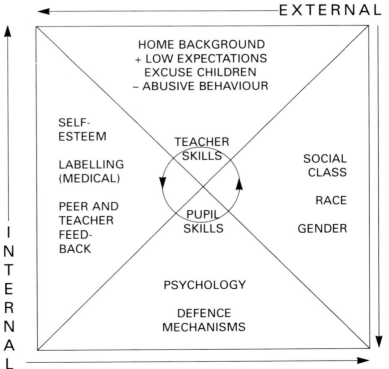

Figure 1:1 Model of factors influencing emotional and behavioural difficulties

In the past many teachers have not been given the opportunity to learn the skills to either recognise that their feelings are connected to the pupils' feelings or to deal with both sets of feelings in a constructive manner. The usual consequence for teachers is a feeling of frustration; they want the children to change their behaviour so that the children themselves get better outcomes. They are concerned about the destructive climate that is created for the rest of the class as they know it impedes learning, but the usual strategies of sanctions, reasoning, punishments and exclusions just do not seem to work for these children. With the combination of frustration with, and concern for, the children it is not surprising that teachers also begin to feel angry with the children.

Given that the anger of the children is to do with pain, the anger of the teacher will not work. This is why punishment, exclusions or other sanctions also do not work. They merely add to the child's pain. (See Fontana, 1985 and Train, 1993). The work of Dreikurs (1968) indicates that all disturbing or unacceptable behaviour in the classroom is an expression of a sense of inferiority (see Adler, 1927,1930). What we are recommending is that in order to address the pain we address through a skills training programme the things that either cause the pain or make it worse.

The three elements in this are: the relationship with the teacher and the classroom environment which can cause pain through failure; the relationships with other children where pain can be inflicted by name calling, being ignored, being belittled or being singled out because you are different in some way; and pain caused by home circumstances.

When the teacher becomes more skilled at dealing with their own and the child's feelings, and the peer group are taught to cause each other less pain, then the child is more able to deal with the pain that is theirs at home. As the pain decreases, then the expression of anger subsides and behaviour changes.

Children in school usually demonstrate that they have emotional difficulties by continuously behaving in an unacceptable way and by not responding to the usual strategies that work for the others. When this happens the first step is to look at the causes of that problem, in order to gain some understanding of the motivation of the child.

The causes of emotional and behavioural difficulties explored below are the ones most commonly and understandably offered by teachers to explain the behavioural problems they encounter. A critique of some of the explanations is outlined below. This is linked with the skills teachers need to deal with difficult behaviour.

Internal and external factors

There has been a long-standing debate about the influence of nature and nurture in education. It would seem that when a child with emotional and behavioural difficulty presents problems in school then there is a tendency to blame both internal (medical and psychological) and external (sociological) factors. It is common for such children to be assessed as being affected by some or all of the following external factors:

● socio-economic group: such influences as poverty, social class, ethnic group and gender might be seen as affecting the child's behaviour;

- home background: a history of physical or sexual abuse, a lack of good parenting, or serial relationships might also play a part in emotional problems;
- accident and circumstance: recent death of a parent or sibling, parental separation, or an illness or disability of someone close to the child may be having an influence on the problem.

There may also be a whole set of other factors which are considered to be important in assessing the child's emotional and behavioural problems. These are internal factors within the child. The ones most commonly referred to by teachers are:

- medical conditions: brain damage, Asperger's syndrome, hyper-activity;
- psychological conditions: low self-esteem, psychotic disorders;
- levels of intelligence; commonly measured by IQ tests, reading age tests, learning difficulty checklists.

These internal and external factors will be addressed in this chapter under the following headings:

- social class and ethnic grouping;
- level of self esteem;
- psychology.

Social class and ethnic grouping as a cause

Social class and ethnic grouping are still seen by many teachers to be the cause of the behavioural difficulty. (For a summary see recent research in Charlton and David, 1989.) Social class and ethnic grouping, then, are interpreted by some teachers as contributing to a deficit within the child.

Home background

'What do you expect coming from that household, her mother was like that.'
'He's a McFey, they never do any good at school.'

A reason often cited for children behaving in ways that teachers find difficult, is the behaviour that is learnt and considered acceptable in the home. The assumption here is that the reason for the child's behaviour, good and bad, lies inside the home and outside the classroom. Teachers, when faced with children from home backgrounds which they deem to be 'good', attribute good attitudes towards learning and school to the home, and thus have high expectations of both behaviour and academic success. The reverse is also true so that information about parental separation, siblings' imprisonment, new baby in the family, give rise to the expectation that the pupil will behave badly or that their work will suffer as a result of the home circumstances. Given that Rosenthal and Jacobson (1968) showed that teacher expectation can influence the performance and behaviour, it then becomes difficult to separate out cause and effect. Teachers' expectation that there will be bad behaviour as a result of bad parenting, either based on assumptions about parenting because of social class, or because of new information about parental circumstances, is conveyed to the pupils through a process of teacher feedback to the pupil, both verbal and non verbal.

This feedback can be as subtle as the amount of time the teacher gives the pupil to answer a question before going on to another student, or it can amount to more blatant statements such as 'You carry on like that you'll end up in prison like your brother'. The effect of both sets of feedback is to alter the pupil's self image from one which says 'I am a worthwhile person and so it's worth trying' to 'I'll never be any good so why bother'.

In conclusion then, to a certain extent the home background is important, in so much as the previously learned behaviours took place in the home. However, the home background is not important in relation to the classroom based stimulus.

Whilst information about home background may help to explain something about the child's frame of mind, skill level or pattern of behaviour, it is essential that it remains just one source of information as to possible motivation. The difficult behaviour happens in the classroom, between the teacher and the child, or between child and child. The pupil is the one who can tell us most clearly about their motivation and their feelings. This tendency to look for home background as a cause is an indication of teacher defensiveness and of their reluctance to look at their own behaviour, feelings and part in the relationship.

Teacher attitude

Home background and social class are often offered as the explanation for difficult behaviour and as a result a child may be labelled 'deviant'.

The evidence from detailed observational research shows a different picture, one in which the institutional norms and expectations mean that those children who cannot fit these expectations are labelled by teachers as difficult or deviant. The way in which norms in schools work against working class children and contribute to deviance has been well documented by Hargreaves (1975), Galloway and Goodwin (1979, 1987), and Willis (1977) who showed that a certain amount of deviance was due to the conflict between white working class norms and school norms.

The macro elements of deprivation: poor estates, inner city areas, rural areas, have an impact on the way that teachers view children and shape their attitude. It can lead to the 'you can't do that with my children' syndrome that both the authors have experienced during their extensive in-service work with teachers. Teachers will often say, with the most positive motives, 'You can't teach that to children from this area'. During the introduction of the National Curriculum, one of the authors was working as an Advisory Teacher for National Curriculum Assessment. One skill teachers were often heard to cite as being inappropriate to teach to children from 'bad estates' was joined-up handwriting. On reflection there is clearly no causal relationship between socio-economic background and an ability to join up handwriting. However, in the minds of the teachers requiring joined-up handwriting would be putting too many burdens on already overburdened children.

These teachers were in fact acting from positive motives, trying to protect their children, but the effect was to deny the children an opportunity to learn and be successful in a required skill, which they will need later on to get jobs. In fact the importance for students with emotional and behavioural difficulties of having access to the same curriculum as everyone else cannot be overestimated.

The research evidence on self-esteem as outlined below shows that pupils with emotional and behavioural difficulties have a low self-esteem (Lund 1987). One of the factors connected with this would seem to be the need all students in special schools feel and that is to be the same as everyone else. This includes the need to know that they have access to the same curriculum as everyone else, (Galloway, 1987). These pupils cannot have academic success unless they believe that their curriculum is the same as everyone else's. Teachers need to ensure that their desire to protect children because of their background experiences outside of school does not lead to either a lowering of expectations or a narrowing of the curriculum.

The problem many teachers have in coping with the notion of difficult behaviour exhibited by intelligent students from middle class backgrounds is another indicator of the link between social class and emotional and behavioural difficulty in many teachers' minds.

Teachers have reported to us accounts of their colleagues expressing difficulty in accepting that it is possible for intelligent children from 'good homes' (sometimes where the parents are teachers), to carry out acts of vandalism and graffiti and for this behaviour to be an expression of an emotional difficulty. Teachers seem to think that if pupils are intelligent then they should be able to behave 'normally', no matter what emotional difficulties they have. The research by Chessum (1980) supports this. Our assertion is that teachers expect and in some way excuse the same behaviour in pupils from working class backgrounds.

It is possible that the difficult behaviour of the intelligent pupil, the pupil from a stable home, the good learner, the pupil from a middle class or privileged background does start to raise uncomfortable feelings for the teacher, that this could be their child. When there is nothing else to blame, when it is clearly not the background of the child, then teachers may need to start to question their own teaching style. This may be uncomfortable for them; however, it is positive from our point of view.

Galloway *et al* (1982, 1985), Galloway and Goodwin (1979, 1987) powerfully argue that since not everyone from low socio-economic backgrounds has emotional and behavioural difficulties, the two factors cannot be inextricably linked. There must be other factors involved which cause more children with low socio-economic backgrounds to be identified as having emotional and behavioural difficulties. The authors note the research findings (Hargreaves *et al,* 1975) which indicate the greater influence of teacher expectations and experiences, of both the teachers' own attitude to school based on their own success and their own prejudices and their resulting behaviours. The authors echo the plea outlined in the 1984 ILEA Hargreaves report, for teachers to change their attitude to students who are disruptive and to see them as students whom the school has failed rather than deviants who become punished and rejected. The work by Hargreaves *et al,* (1975), shows that the behaviour which is construed by teachers as deviant, is shown, when you interview the child concerned, to be very often the result of their reaction to poor teaching. The result of a perceived unfair response by teachers to legitimate complaints by students can easily become an entrenched attitude by the students, because they think, 'What have I got to lose, I'll be blamed anyway'. Similar arguments apply to the issue of race and gender.

Gender

The issue of gender is another example of a factor which cannot in all clear conscience be blamed on the child. On careful analysis we simply cannot wipe out one half of the population and say 'Well boys are like that'. However, when one examines the numbers of girls as opposed to boys in Emotional and Behavioural Difficulties special schools, that is precisely what seems to be going on. In one special school we know of there were seventy boys and one girl.

Whilst the causal relationship is unclear, there is clearly a connection between teacher attention and types of behaviour. Teachers give more attention to boys (Spender, 1982); boys shout out and use aggressive behaviour, and as a result are removed from the classroom either outside the door or outside the entire institution.

Teachers give less time to girls; girls tend to conform, chat to each other, and any expression of unhappiness is in the form of withdrawal or the development of self abusive behaviours such as anorexia. It seems to us that teenage pregnancies are symptoms of the same thing. In our experience it is not so much that the girls do not know how to stop getting pregnant, it is that the girls are internalising feelings of lack of self worth.

One of the big problems that schools need to address in their questioning of gender related behaviours is the gap between what they say they want (the open curriculum) and what they actually reward with attention, and tolerate (hidden curriculum). Research has shown that large amounts of verbal abuse and 'acting out' behaviour are tolerated from boys whilst small amounts of the same behaviour in girls are stamped on with great institutional force. (Thompson, 1986; Weiner, 1985; Mahoney, 1985; Spender, 1982). The converse is also true: a weeping girl will be given time to sort herself out, tissues, off-the-cuff counselling, a trip to the girls loo with a mate, and her poor work will be excused and seen as due to 'her time of the month'. A weeping boy, over infant age, however, throws most teachers into a state of consternation: he will usually be expected to pull himself together and get back down to work; no allowance will be made for his emotional state.

We recognise, however, that changing teacher behaviour is not easy. The prejudices that teachers seem to be operating when they make assumptions about boys are the results of societal norms, of conditioning, which is why it is crucial for teachers to become aware of their own feelings about pupils. One useful way to do this is to use the appraisal system. Teachers can invite a trusted colleague to observe them teaching, and for the colleague to note down, for example, the amount of time and type of attention given to boys as opposed to girls. (The Genderwatch (1987) pack has lots of helpful checklists).The depressing truth that we have found in our observations supports the initial work carried out by Dale Spender in 1982, which shows that not only do teachers give about 70 per cent of their attention to boys, but also when teachers try really hard to give equal time, they manage to achieve a 60/40 split in favour of the boys who complain!

There is an interesting set of contradictions that operate in most schools in that on the one hand teachers behave as if boys do not have feelings, whilst on the other they experience, and even tolerate, the clear expression of feelings in the form of play fighting. They then have rules which say no fighting or hitting, thereby suppressing the only outlet at present for boys to express the way that they feel. This is not an argument for allowing hitting, it is an argument for teaching the boys how to express their feelings, and to take more responsibility for challenging, hitting and fighting. For example, teacher behaviour can be used to remonstrate with the on-looking peer group for not helping two fighting boys to overcome their problems in another way.

In addition to an initial observation exercise the recommendation throughout this book is for teachers to:

- examine the rules for the hidden and open curriculum;
- examine the structure of the school and classroom;
- ensure that the boys' behaviour is actually saying that which it is assumed to say, (teachers need to use checking out language);
- teach the boys how to express their feelings verbally instead of only being able to resort to violence and verbal abuse.

Race

The behaviour of working class boys is more likely to be found unacceptable in school institutions, and that of working class Afro-Caribbean boys the most unacceptable.

It seems to the authors that Afro-Caribbean behaviours, especially non verbal, are the very ones interpreted in the conformity norms in schools as being insolent, sly, aggressive, manipulative and non-co-operative. We therefore see a connection between this teacher interpretation and the numbers of Afro-Caribbean students in the specialist schools and units for emotional and behavioural difficulties, which are totally disproportionate to the population distribution. (See Cooper, Smith and Upton 1990).

The research evidence for this is put forward by Tomlinson, Taylor and Hegarty, in Cohen and Cohen's book of collected readings, (1987).

The emphasis on style and rapport between Afro-Caribbean peers is one that is not appreciated by many teachers, yet research evidence shows (Furlong, 1984; Fuller, 1982) that such cultural norms are not synonymous with an anti-school attitude, although this does not mean that they are going to conform to non-academic school norms. It is teachers who make this assumption and in this sense create the problem for Afro-Caribbean students, in a determination to 'break their will'. In the experience of the authors this is a battle that teachers will not win, and is one that should not be embarked upon if the recommendations about self-esteem in *Pupils with Problems* (D.F.E. 1994) are to be taken seriously.

Some teachers see a connection between ethnicity and aggression.

It could be said that all of these pupils have a genetic defect which predisposes them towards violence, an argument clearly stated by some politically motivated groups. However, to educationists this argument is irrational. Or we could look to both social and institutional norms and expectations as being the reason for certain ethnic groups to tend to act out in an aggressive manner. If teachers were to ask and find out what it is that the Afro-Caribbean pupil is really feeling, they may well find that the motivation, thinking and feeling of this student is actually different to the interpretation placed on it by teachers. One way forward would be for institutions to become more flexible in the behaviours they demand. The other would be for the institution to work harder at studying the pupils' perspective of school in the way that Hargreaves *et al* (1967, 1975), Tatum (1982), Cronk (1987) and Woods (1990) have demonstrated.

In conclusion then, it can be said that school norms can contribute to creating a problem for some students particularly those from working class and Afro-Caribbean backgrounds (Galloway and Goodwin, 1987).

Norms and teacher expectations

The evidence that schools themselves can and do make a difference to levels of expulsion and referral and that they can change their norms to alter these rates is overwhelming, (Rutter *et al,* 1979; Mortimore *et al,* 1988; HMI, 1977, 1979, 1985; Reynolds, 1976, 1984; Elton, DES 1989; Galloway, 1985). Statements made by teachers in staff rooms about social class being a cause therefore need to be challenged. So too do the assumptions made about the motivation of students.

Whilst there is evidence showing that some schools are creating the problem (Elton, 1989; Galloway and Goodwin, 1987) and that where schools have taken this seriously they have started to solve the problem, (Reynolds,1985; Hopkins, Hargreaves, School Effectiveness research; Charlton and David, 1990), there is also evidence that more and more students are being excluded (ILEA, 1990; Merrick and Manuel, 1991; Pyke,1991). This must mean that some schools are simply ignoring or refusing to look at the research evidence showing their part in the problem and are continuing to blame the child.

We have explored the way in which schools as institutions are inconsistent in their demands and expectations of different groups of students according to their perceived background. We have made it clear that these are norms of the institution which are not openly declared. Indeed, people may not even be aware of them or the way in which they are influencing their beliefs and behaviours. There are other norms or ways of doing things that are not clearly expressed, and are therefore part of the hidden curriculum of the school.

The norm which the authors feel is most damaging to children and results in them being labelled as having emotional and behavioural difficulties is that which relates to repentance and remorse after an incident of bad behaviours. The expectations in relation to incidents of poor behaviour include indicators of remorse such as:

- lowering of eyes or saying sorry;
- offering an explanation.

Lowering of eyes may also be expected as a sign of respect for the one who is correcting the pupil, and a failure to do so may be interpreted as lack of respect, insolence, or deliberate defiance.

Equally, meeting eye contact may be seen as a sign of respect and recognition of taking responsibility for the poor behaviour, which is why teachers are sometimes heard to say (or shout) things like 'Look at me when I'm talking to you!'

A response to rational argument is also expected in the shape of both expressions of contrition and acceptance of the poor behaviour together with a commitment to change that behaviour.

Whilst we would agree that the latter points constitute the outcome all of us would like and should be working towards, we maintain that some pupils with emotional and behavioural difficulties do not have the emotional wherewithal to do all of these things at once, and need to be taught these skills for expressing their perspective. Additionally we note the number of interpretations that are residing in the hidden curriculum and regard it as crucial that such interpretations are checked out with hard evidence. In our view it is essential that all schools, primary, secondary and special make continuous efforts to:

- consider the hidden curricula norms that may be at work in their institution;
- incorporate the ones which staff can agree on in terms of importance into the school behaviour policy;
- agree to work at removing the ones not agreed on;
- consider ways of teaching the pupils the skills they need to keep to the norms and values expressed in the behaviour policy.

Self-esteem as a cause

For all students and children, but particularly those with emotional and behavioural difficulties, there is a theoretical framework which not only explains behaviour but also offers a model for changing behaviour in a whole class setting. This framework is based on self-esteem theory. (Coopersmith, 1967; Hamachek, 1987; Burns, 1982). Most teachers will recognise the fact that children with emotional and behavioural difficulties feel badly about themselves. It has been demonstrated through research that these children do have a low self-esteem. (Lund, 1988). If we fit self-esteem into the hierarchy of needs that Maslow (1962) established, it becomes clear that self-esteem is a basic need, and that once the needs for food, water, security and belonging are met, the next most important is self-esteem.

If children with emotional and behavioural difficulties have this low self-esteem, and self-esteem is a need, then teachers must address how they are going to meet their need for that esteem to be raised.

Self-esteem theory recognises that humans know who and what they are through a series of messages or feedback.

I am not who I think I am.
I am not who you think I am.
I am who I think you think I am.

We know what we are like because others tell us, that is to say they give us negative and positive feedback. Coopersmith's research (1967) showed that there are three groups of people in our lives who are highly influential in shaping our view of ourselves through giving us this feedback.

They are: our parents, our peers and our teachers. Coopersmith found that of those who were significant to pupils the peer group and the teacher feedback were two thirds of the influence in shaping self-esteem, whilst the parents' influence was only one third. This was found to be especially true of academic self-esteem which is the major influence on academic achievement.

The research evidence shows (Gordan, 1974; Jones and Jones, 1990) that when peer feedback is combined with teacher feedback then behaviour is changed. This is because the two thirds outweighs the one third parental influence. One of the problems in many classrooms is that the ethos of not saying how you feel, of not talking socially, of only getting on with 'on task' work, means that pupils do not know for sure how their peers feel about them. They can only guess through non-verbal feedback, and that guess is likely to be inaccurate. Additionally the peers do not actually come to know the pupil. They only know them through their behaviour or reputation and the image the pupil is projecting rather than the real person, so the likelihood of the feedback being negative is very high. In fact the evidence from self-esteem theory (Coopersmith, 1967; Hamachek, 1987; Burns, 1982; Purkey, 1984) shows that teachers can make a difference to children's behaviour if they teach all the children in a class to give positive and realistic feedback.

Many teachers have expressed to us their feelings of frustration about children's self-esteem. They think that nothing that they can say in school will be of any effect because of the overpowering nature of the negative feedback that pupils get at home.

Our experience shows that as teachers we can help children, even those with very negative feedback at home, to change their view of themselves and subsequently to change their behaviour.

Self-esteem is a measurement of self worth. We have a high self-esteem if the way we see ourselves, our self image (formed by the impression we have of other's thoughts about us), is close to the way we would like to be; our ideal self. From the outside no-one can tell what a person's self-esteem is because they do not know about their self-image or their ideal self. Thus an Olympic swimmer may have a low self-esteem because their ideal self is one who can swim faster than their current performance.

A low self-esteem is the result of the feedback received creating a self image which is very different from the person's ideal self. The self image can be changed by providing feedback which is more positive and by ensuring that the person's ideal self is realistic. As the self image and the ideal self become closer, self-esteem, or the way we feel about ourselves is raised.

Classrooms where information about the way we think others see us and our ideal selves are shared, and become part of the open curricular information, are ones where self image and ideal self can be influenced and ultimately changed through feedback. Classrooms where such information is hidden stand no chance of influencing self-esteem through peer feedback. Children are entirely reliant on teacher feedback and undeclared, covert peer cues, which in all probability are misread.

Importance of feedback to self-esteem

The amount and type of feedback influences the pupil's academic image and self-esteem (Burns 1982). Coopersmith found that giving too little feedback is in itself damaging as the pupil assumes that this lack of feedback is because they are not worthy of your attention. Bad feedback therefore makes pupils feel important and is better for their feelings of self-worth than no feedback at all. (Burns, 1982; Lawrence, 1987; Hamachek, 1987).

The way children feel about themselves affects their ability to form social relationships with their peers and their teachers. (Hamachek, 1987; Canfield and Wells, 1976). Children who have received feedback that tells them that they are good people to know will have confidence in making social contacts. A person with a healthy social self-esteem will think, 'I am a nice person to know, which means that someone will want to know me'. Any social rebuff will be attributed to a temporary mood or other understandable reason on the part of the other or themselves. 'He doesn't want to play because he/I is/am a bit grumpy today'.

However, children who feel bad about themselves and have a low self-esteem are likely to see the same social rebuff as permanent and destructive, 'He doesn't ever want to be my friend because I'm such an awful person to be with. I don't deserve any friends.' This destructive feeling is then hidden away under the child's defences and results in them hitting out at the other child or becoming a 'loner.' The research evidence which supports these illustrations is gathered together in Hamachek (1987), Burns (1982), Brookover (1962, 1967), whilst the work of Lawrence – his extensive research projects are summarised in his book of 1987 – shows a British application of the American research.

In the same way, a child may hear any correction from the teacher as a total rejection of themselves. A comment such as 'It's a bit messy' is taken on board as 'I'm such a mess, I never get anything right, no wonder that the teacher hates me and I'm always in trouble'. The resultant behaviour might be destructive, aggressive, a lack of motivation, sullen looks or over-talkative and noisy interruptions. The defence chosen will be whatever makes that child, temporarily, feel better about themselves.

Medical conditions

Low self-esteem can also be caused by having medical problems. This is primarily caused by the negative feedback that children with medical conditions get from their peers.

There is a problem in trying to put a name to the sorts of medical and psychological conditions involved in those identified as children with emotional and behavioural difficulties. As the Underwood Report (Ministry of Education, 1955) demonstrates, an attempt to define emotional and behavioural difficulties in medical terminology tends to end up as a list of symptoms and not a list of conditions. For example, nervous habit behaviour, organic and psychotic disorders. Even when medical labels are attributed, like autism and Asperger's Syndrome, further investigation shows that the label is a shorthand for a cluster of symptoms, such as withdrawal, inability to relate to others, difficulty in sitting still. As Cooper, Smith and Upton point out (1994), a great deal of time can be spent on making sure that the right label is attached to the child rather than focusing on practical help for the child; for example teaching them to read. This is the reason why we feel that there is little point in pursuing this route, except to help teachers to gain some understanding and empathy with the motivation of the child. If the child has epilepsy and quite often has headaches, then a knowledge of the medical condition might allow the teacher to empathise and think, 'If I had a headache then I too might be snappy'.

The idea that children with 'medical conditions' that give rise to behavioural difficulties need educating in another institution, for example in a 'school for the delicate', is one that has been challenged over the last two decades. It is quite usual these days for even young children with fairly severe asthma, diabetes or epilepsy to be given their medical treatment in school and for them to be educated 'normally' alongside their peers. Indeed separate provision could not possibly match the need for asthma these days, yet the same attitude of 'integration is best' is not so readily observed when one sees children who teachers deem to have 'longterm behaviour problems'. These children are much more likely to be pushed towards the segregated setting.

Nevertheless even those in the integrated setting need help if they are not to be picked on and bullied or become 'mothered' by their peers.

If children have epilepsy, diabetes, asthma, a colostomy or disturbed sleep patterns then it is important for the class teacher or tutor to create an environment where all the students can talk about personal and medical difficulties without embarrassment. The aim here is for the teacher to teach the individual with the medical problem, and their peers to own and share the problem, point out the difficulties, ask for help, goal set and action plan. Ideally this will take place alongside all their peers who have health related issues e.g. smoking, weight, exercise, and will set up expectations that they do not hide the problem and pretend it isn't there. The action plan itself can be specifically designed to include 'what I'm going to do for me' and 'what I am going to do to help someone else', i.e. buddying (see McNamara in Harrison and Edwards, 1994).

Child development

The medical terminology used by some teachers as a cry for help in dealing with difficult behaviour needs careful analysis as it so easily leads to unproductive, possibly destructive labelling. For example a teacher may say: 'I need some classroom support for Ian, I think he is possibly brain damaged.' After further questioning it may transpire that the student rolls around on the carpet and cannot yet ride a bicycle, and is five years old. Whilst this behaviour in a fifteen year old child would probably cause most teachers and parents some concern, for a child in a reception class to be behaving this way is not unusual.

What one sees here are developmental issues. It is not unusual for normal children when bored to roll on the carpet, and to develop at different rates, typically focusing on one skill, e.g. learning to be at school. This leaves no focus for bike riding. For example one girl we know had a high reading age and was an excellent swimmer but she did not ride her bike until she was eight years old. The teacher who was using the term 'brain damage' was using it to describe behaviour that she found difficult to deal with and to account for. Careful observation revealed that the child was bored, this was not a 'within-child' medical problem but a teacher curriculum delivery problem.

Psychology as a cause

Learning difficulty or behaviour difficulty?

Many of the children with emotional and behavioural difficulties have associated learning difficulties. This provides teachers who wish to use more positive praise for these students with a dilemma. When the behaviour is poor you might wish to give positive feedback about the academic achievement. If there are learning difficulties then the feedback if accurate is not very positive, if inaccurate, is recognised by the child as being false praise. The teacher's frustration as to how or what to praise is then clear. This might be why so many 'star charts' fail. There is nothing for which to give a star!

One important question for those teachers who have children who present both difficulties is that of which came first. Did the learning difficulty cause the failure which then led to a poor self image and so poor behaviour followed? This has been a view widely accepted by teachers. The remedial action therefore required was to provide the child with learning successes, often through a small steps programme which then allowed the child positive reinforcements. This would lead to better behaviour. Again, teachers working hard to employ small steps programmes were frustrated at the lack of influence on the behaviour as well as the slow progress in terms of increased learning. This is historically where many of the extra resources for special needs have been employed, in support teachers, ancillary helpers and special placements.

The authors think that the opposite view should also be examined.

Children may exhibit poor behaviour when they first enter school because of a pattern established in pre-school years, or it may be that they experienced a negative incident in the early days of their schooling. This may be as seemingly trivial as the teacher 'ticking mummy off' for standing at the wrong door when collecting them, tripping on the school step on their first day, finding their drawer or peg is the only one without a name card. The incidents are experienced as an emotion, they are not rationalised. Teachers can identify that for them too, feelings block the ability to learn or function rationally. If a teacher bumps their car on the way to school, concentrating on their job becomes very difficult. Whereas in this situation colleagues readily respond and show understanding of this phenomenon and make appropriate allowances, this is not always the case for young children. As a result of being preoccupied by their feelings they may show an inability to concentrate. If reprimanded this may then lead to poor behaviour.

The poor behaviour might affect the child's view of themselves as a not very good person. If the poor behaviour is related to the classroom then the picture forming for the child is that they are not very good in school. The poor school image then influences the way in which a child is able to learn. If you believe you are 'no good at being at school' then there is little point in risking trying things out, little point in working hard or even relating well to others in the school. This view might seem similar but the implications for remedial action are quite different. If this is the case then the self image of the child needs to be altered and this is where the efforts of the teacher need to be targeted.

We believe that the first approach to children with emotional and behavioural difficulties who have learning difficulties should be to address their feelings about themselves. The raising of their self esteem through counselling approaches is a prerequisite to any changes in behaviour and should precede any attempt to gain successful feedback through progress in their learning.

Defence mechanisms

Self consistency theory (Burns, 1982; Allport, 1950; Rogers, 1959) shows that once a self concept is formed, no matter how good or bad, all human beings will try to protect it. People will go to great lengths, even to self delusion, to protect their feelings of self worth. Even when someone has a poor self concept, they will avoid feeling anything else that will make them feel even worse, so what people do is defend themselves. William James (1890), one of the earliest writers on self-concept, said 'with no attempt there can be no failure, with no failure no humiliation.' You either flee, go inside yourself and cut off from the world (for example elective mutes), or you fight, displaying anger and aggression. In our experience it is easier to deal with fight behaviours than it is with flight!

The behaviour the children are displaying is behaviour which is defending the way they feel about themselves. Defending oneself against attack is understandable (Train, 1993) and teachers who learn to view behaviour this way will find that it is also easier to be forgiving. They will also be able to see such aggression as an expression of a vulnerable person trying to defend themselves rather than a personal attack on teachers.

One statement commonly heard in staff rooms to explain difficult behaviour is that it is 'attention seeking.' It is our view that this is also a defence mechanism. Coopersmith (1967) recognised that we all need to be given attention. His research established that a lack of some attention is in fact more damaging than negative attention. This brings a new perspective to the issue of attention seeking. Coopersmith says that the need for attention is a drive common to all humans. Pupils who are attention seeking, therefore, are trying to get one of their basic needs met. They can be helped fairly easily if structures such as pair work and group work are introduced which enable all pupils in the class to give each other attention.

A case study outlined below illustrates the way that a defence mechanism might work, and the difference teacher response could make.

When a teacher is faced with a child like Jody who has just thrown an empty glass bottle at another child, and Jody refuses to say anything, it is likely that the situation will escalate to one where the child is disciplined. She may even be suspended for dangerous behaviour which she will not explain and this refusal to co-operate will probably be interpreted as dumb insolence. If a skilful teacher intervenes, it may transpire, as a result of careful listening on the teacher's part, that Jody's experiences at home are that confessions are beaten out of her, and punishments of a violent nature result from that confession.

It is not surprising that parents do this in the light of recent revelations of societal methods of extracting information which have led to unsound convictions. It is similarly not surprising that Jody refuses to say anything, nor is it so very surprising that she throws the bottle. She acts in a violent way when she is feeling hurt because another child has shared their prize stickers with everyone else except Jody and violence is the only way she knows of expressing her anger. Many teachers on learning this information about Jody, may say that she needs to learn self-control. Of course her behaviour does need to change, but the specific classroom based incident was one in which she felt hurt.

Her pattern, which had been learned in the home, was used since she knew no other way of behaving. The defence mechanism is to be violent when feeling hurt; this is because anger is usually a secondary emotion covering the primary emotion of pain. It is operating for teachers in exactly the same way when they see red and really shout at pupils. The skilful and constructive thing for teachers to do at this point is either to declare their primary feeling to the pupils and say clearly 'I feel hurt when you do that', because this is modelling the kind of reflective behaviour they want in pupils; or to shout and then apologise explaining that the reason for being so very angry was that they felt hurt: again this models the behaviour that they want.

If the defence mechanism is interpreted as defiant or deliberate behaviour the person concerned will probably be punished, which to them may seem unfair and they are unlikely to change their behaviour in the future. As noted earlier, a common expectation of teachers is that when students behave badly or do something to hurt someone else the students are expected to show contrition and remorse. When they do not, both teachers and judges alike assume that the person concerned is not sorry and that they:

- do not understand the difference between right and wrong, that there is a cognitive, learning problem and that they need to be taught a lesson;
- that they are hardened and need a harsh punishment;
- or that they are mentally ill, or deviant. Many medical labels may be used here which as was noted earlier are only symptom descriptors of people who behave in ways that we find difficult to understand.

Whatever the explanation, the conclusion is that they need harsh punishments in order to make them understand or respond and make them feel sorry; in particular to make them feel sorry for their victim. The reason why this does not work is because the inability to feel and express remorse is more likely to be to do with the inability to feel anything at all.

The need, according to our assessment, is a programme of skills training at a time when Jody is not feeling vulnerable, (that is to say hurt and threatened), when Jody and the others in the class can explore and learn new behaviour for expressing feelings. The role-plays outlined in chapter six on feelings, which help pupils to say 'I feel hurt,' are designed for this purpose.

Inability to feel as a cause

It is a normal human reaction to split off from the hurting part of ourselves. However, when we do this we split off from our ability to feel anything at all. (Rogers, 1961; Dreikurs, 1968; Balson, 1982).

One common reaction from people who are damaged is that they feel so badly already they cannot tolerate anything else that increases that bad feeling and so they put up defences in order not to hear anything. In this way they reduce the chances of being hurt any more.

The most destructive thing about this is that by shutting off from the negative, they also shut off from the one thing that would redress the balance, so they cannot feel good feelings, they cannot hear praise or good information. What they are doing is defending their present low self-esteem, which is why we recommend work on feedback as an initial step, in this cycle of feelings of negative self worth.

In addition such youngsters cannot empathise with others. This means that they can easily be bullies or can damage others; having been bullied themselves they have had plenty of opportunities to learn how to bully others. Bullying behaviour by teachers merely adds to the negative model. What these pupils are in effect saying is that they will not allow anyone to reach them, to touch them emotionally and they will not allow themselves to have caring feelings for others in case they get hurt in the way they have been before. The challenge for us in the teaching profession is to learn how to reach in over the shell and help the child to believe that teachers are really there for them, that they can trust teachers and that neither teachers nor the pupil's peers will hurt them. Teacher behaviour which is assertive, which disapproves of the pupil's behaviour whilst remaining warmly empathetic to the individual, is important because it is offering a new way of behaving both to that individual child and to the whole class.

To return to the beginning then, our thesis is that emotionally and behaviourally disturbed pupils are pupils who are damaged. Their behaviours are not to do with manipulation and power, they are to do with protection and the need to feel something. Many students report on the inability to escape patterns of behaviour because this is the only way they get peer response and attention. Such students need help.

Clearly teachers do not have the time to counsel every pupil with emotional and behavioural difficulties in their class, but other pupils do, and these pupils are there for the damaged ones at times when the teacher is not: breaks, before and after school, in the corridors. Most pupils are already very skilled at reading teachers' and adults' non-verbal communications, hidden signals, hidden rules, so it's fairly easy for them to learn to do this overtly. That is to say, to learn the skills of being counsellors for each other.

For pupils and children who are damaged then, punishments and sanctions are inappropriate. What we recommend is healing through a therapeutic environment.

CHAPTER 2

Skills for Teaching Pupils with Emotional and Behavioural Difficulties

How a change in teacher attitude can be effected

We have demonstrated in the previous chapter that a positive attitude from teachers towards emotionally and behaviourally disturbed pupils is vital if they are to support their pupils in their attempts to change their behaviour. It would be helpful if all teachers could move to an attitudinal position where they can see that some difficulties are caused by school norms and expectations which do not fit with social class and ethnic group behavioural norms. This is an in-service issue that raises the question of whether it is possible for teachers to change the way in which they behave in the classroom. Many attempts have been made to change curriculum delivery over the years by introducing new ideas through in-service training, legislation and management pressure. Many teachers have resisted those pressures to change and changing teacher attitudes has proved to be very difficult to achieve, some would say impossible to achieve. The authors disagree.

Research on teacher belief systems shows that teachers with a predisposition to change, that is, positive attitudes, are likely to try new practices and change their methods. This might lead to an assumption that only teachers with positive attitudes, who already have a belief system that supports changes will be able or willing to respond. This would mean children with emotional and behavioural difficulties are destined to be taught by very few teachers who will be able to help them. Our experience of working with very many teachers leads us to believe that although there are teachers with a predisposition to be open to new ideas and changes in practice, there are many who are not.

It has been shown (Hamachek, 1987; Burns, 1982) that teachers with a healthy self-esteem are more able to foster self-esteem in their pupils. It is possible to view teachers as victims of their past; adopting teaching strategies which they themselves suffered, and which lowered their self-esteem, because those are the only strategies they are aware of for dealing with difficult behaviour. The constant sense of failure that such teachers experience when using methods that often humiliate rather than heal students with difficulties, or the exhaustion teachers feel as they continually battle to negotiate with such students, often lowers their own self-esteem. This may well result in very negative, self-defensive attitudes. What is happening in this case is that teachers too are using sophisticated defence mechanisms which may be one reason why they find it hard to deal with children who are doing the same.

For teacher trainers and managers of schools this is very significant. It becomes clear that there are two aspects to bringing about changes in teachers' behaviour when dealing with emotionally and behaviourally disturbed children.

– Firstly they need to have their own self-esteem raised through success and positive approval. To do this they need new skills which will provide them with the success which they have previously not had.

– Secondly, there needs to be an attitude change which will bring about a predisposition to try out new approaches to children with emotional and behavioural difficulties.

Working with these teachers has demonstrated to us that by training through a skills programme and thus giving teachers helpful skills, their attitude changes. We have found that the resulting attitude change ensures that the newly acquired skills are more likely to be used and developed after the training programme has finished. There are many teachers in school already with positive attitudes and strategies for children with emotional and behavioural difficulties, who might be struggling against a tide of others who are far more negative. For them our experience shows that, if they help a colleague through giving positive feedback and support perhaps through modelling, to have some of the skills we believe to be most important, then that colleague will be able to shift their underlying attitude.

Some teachers who have had a negative experience when dealing with children with emotional and behavioural difficulties may have developed an associated negative attitude. We believe that if these teachers are helped to develop particular skills then they will acquire a more positive attitude. It is our belief that behaviour policies alone will not lead to a change in children's behaviour. It is only when managers of schools both recognise the importance of skills training for their teachers and ensure that all their teachers have access to such training, that a whole school approach can be achieved.

When teachers use the appropriate skills, they have reported to us that they prove to be successful. This success in dealing with children with challenging behaviour leads to an increase in the teacher's own self-esteem. Through this mechanism the teacher is more able to implement changes in classroom ethos, curriculum delivery and level of feedback and so support the child's self-esteem.

Skills training for teachers

We need to identify which skills are important for success with emotionally and behaviourally disturbed children.

Outlined below are the skills that we consider important. They have been clustered together under two headings, the first giving an indication of the psychological theory that underpins the skills, behaviourism, and the second being counselling skills. The importance of each skill is highlighted in each of the chapters on practical activities, together with the skills that the pupils need to learn.

Behaviourism

It is important for teachers to remember that the evidence from psychologists is that behaviour is a combination of a response to the immediate stimulus in the classroom together with a replication of previously learned behaviour. We need to examine the contribution of behaviourism because it is the theory that has dominated classroom intervention work in the shape of advice from educational psychologists and books on the subject of managing difficult behaviour. In addition, the D.F.E. 1994 document on *Pupils with Problems* recommends certain procedures through stages one to three which are drawn from behaviour modification theory.

The authors take the view that it is necessary to use:

- observation to generate a description of the actual behaviour and so eradicate the use of labels or 'home background';
- detailed recording of frequency and intensity of behaviour so that discussions about degrees of difficulty are as objective as possible;
- reflections on antecedents and consequences around the behaviour so that the teacher behaviour and classroom or school environment are considered;
- behaviour management programmes which must also be discussed with students so that they can begin to see and understand their own patterns of behaviour and to feel that they have some control over them.

Being specific about behaviour

One of the strategies recommended in the D.F.E. document 1994, is that of the model for analysing behaviour derived from learning theory (Skinner, 1974, 1968, and Bandura, 1969, 1977) which is known as the A, B, C: Antecedent, Behaviour, and Consequence. For more information on the theory behind these recommendations, see Westmacott and Cameron, 1983; Wheldall, 1987; 1992; Wheldall and Merrett 1984, and Sheldon 1982.

The application of such a model is only helpful if the behaviour itself can be identified, and elements of it quantified. For example, when a teacher feels a child is attention seeking or a student is being disruptive, that teacher can then be encouraged to either: observe that child or student themselves, or get a colleague to do the same. As a result of these observations specific behaviours will probably be identified such as:

'chewing a pencil, consuming one a week',

'getting out of seat – 15 times in one lesson',

'jabbing neighbours with a ruler – 85 times in half an hour'.

Having the behaviour identified and named as one specific behaviour with elements of duration and frequency attached allows everyone, child, parent, teacher, head teacher, educational psychologist, to be sure that they are talking about the same thing. Without such clear behavioural statements there is a strong likelihood that discussions will be based on judgements and interpretations, for example; deviance, defiance, attention seeking. These terms are problematical as they attribute motivation to children and students without checking out their accuracy and are entirely dependant on individual teachers' value systems. One teacher's disruption can be another's challenge. For example: one teacher may interpret chewing gum as deliberate defiance but choose to ignore racist language, whilst another may interpret aggressive derogatory sexual comments from a boy addressed to a girl as bullying and be relatively unmoved by drinking and eating in class.

For those who feel that behaviourism is mechanistic, we would argue that it provides systematic objectivity which can only be helpful in the face of the problems for students engendered by interpretative, judgmental labels.

What such behavioural statements also do is to confirm that the behaviours are classroom bound. Research evidence shows over and again that the behaviours teachers find most difficult to deal with are TOOT – Talking Out Of Turn – and getting out of your seat.

The Elton Report, 1989, recorded the percentage of secondary teachers reporting that they had to deal with difficult types of behaviour in the classroom at least once in a week. The results confirmed previous research, and found:

> talking out of turn – 97%
> calculated idleness or work avoidance – 87%
> hindering other pupils work – 86%
> not being punctual – 82%
> making unnecessary non-verbal noise – 77%

These are all group related behaviours, they are not an obvious problem in the home but they are a clear problem in a class of thirty or more.

The need for teachers to learn the skill of being specific about behaviour is clear. It is also the first step in the skill of giving feedback and using the three part message outlined below and to that extent it is a pre-skill.

Being consistent with reward

The research carried out by behaviourist psychologists (Wheldall, 1987), indicates that teachers when commenting on behaviour as opposed to academic achievement, spend most of their time commenting on the behaviour they do not want, on the negative behaviour, and hardly any time praising and reinforcing the behaviour they do want. As a result teachers are reinforcing negative behaviour whereas they need to increase the rewarding of 'good' behaviour and ignore the 'bad' behaviour.

The suggestions from behaviourists at this point are for teachers to select one specific behaviour, as a result of observation, identify the positive behaviour they want instead of the negative one currently being used by the pupil, and reward this behaviour with either tangible items such as sweets or tokens which build up to a reward or privilege valued by the pupil, or social rewards such as smiling.

Many teachers find such an approach problematic; their objections can best be summarised in this way:

- The ideas seem too childish for the secondary classroom – certainly the research evidence shows most effectiveness either in the primary or the special school setting – the work of Wheldall although well documented focuses more on the primary school. (Wheldall and Glynn, 1989; Wheldall and Merrett, 1984, 1992).

- It is too difficult in the secondary setting to persuade up to ten different teachers who teach an individual child to work together in order to get the level of consistency required.

- Teachers have too many students or children in the class to be able to attend to so many different individual programmes. (The special school settings where behaviourism has been used longest have groups of fifteen or less i.e. less than half the size of mainstream classrooms).

- Teachers feel they cannot spend the amount of time required to achieve consistency when they have so much syllabus content to get through. This is an argument put forward by both primary and secondary colleagues teaching the National Curriculum, but is particularly heartfelt from secondary English, History and Science teachers.

Whilst the authors sympathise with the problems outlined above, and agree with the difficulties presented by individual behavioural modification programmes, they feel it is vital that teachers do not dismiss the principles of rewarding on-task behaviour altogether.

It is our view that teachers need to pay careful attention to the power of reward and to make their reward system explicit and achievable for all pupils. They need to increase the amount of praise they give to pupils and look to this as their number one tool in shaping pupils' behaviour. Once teachers have acquired the skill of praising they can use the strategies outlined in the following chapters which are designed for 'whole class work'.

Making rules explicit

At first glance this may not seem like a skill. In order to make classroom rules explicit, teachers do need the skills of reflection upon their own practice. The ability to examine their own underlying beliefs, prejudices and assumptions honestly is the basis for being able to understand why some classroom rules are very important to them and where their low or high tolerance of some behaviours stems from. An honest appraisal of teachers' own values will help them to formulate classroom ground rules which are fundamental to them.

Being clear about rules, routines, expectations and assessment procedures is important for pupils with emotional and behavioural difficulties, as they need to know boundaries. By making all the rules explicit the teacher makes it more possible for such pupils to keep to the rules.

The authors of this book take the view that elements of behaviourism are useful especially when introduced in tandem with theories on motivation, including those of self-esteem.

In our scenario the aim is for everyone to try to modify aspects of their own behaviour, including the teacher; and for everyone in the classroom to be involved in giving rewards, including adult helpers and pupils.

Counselling skills

For teachers to respond appropriately to the issues raised in the previous chapter about teacher expectation and social class, race and gender, is very difficult. Most situations that arise are very complex. This is because the issues are interrelated and bound up in a low self-esteem cycle. The tendency of boys to not talk about their feelings, to use an aggressive defence mechanism which teachers find threatening, means that their bad feelings about themselves are hidden. Teachers need to work very hard at peeling back the layers of this complex behaviour in order to see what the real person underneath is actually feeling and thinking. Teachers are the best people to do this, not experts from outside, because they are there in the environment that is causing the problem, and when the feelings are being actually experienced. Counselling skills for teachers are vital as they are basically skills for unravelling complex feelings.

We have found that counselling skills (Egan, 1975; Bolton, 1979) and Transactional Analysis (Berne, 1964) both have a lot to offer teachers in helping them to understand a different interpretation and motivation and acquiring a different set of skills.

There are two helpful chapters in Delwyn Tattum's book (1989), which address counselling and interpersonal skills.

To explore the way in which these skills can help, consider a typical interchange between pupil and teacher. The pupil says, 'I ain't doing this it's boring,' The teacher may remonstrate, reason, cajole, or shout and become dictatorial.

The teacher on hearing the phrase may well associate it with a whole set of other attitudes, and potential behaviours. The 'ain't doing it' may be associated with a defiant, down tools, non-co-operation set of behaviours, whilst the 'it's boring' may be experienced as a personal rejection of the teacher's efforts and skills, i.e. you have not worked hard enough and you are no good at the job any-way. It is no wonder that teachers react emotionally to these two phrases, and no wonder that students use them, as they will usually get a reaction from the teacher and if they are driven through low self-esteem by a need for some attention – any attention, positive or negative – then the strategy has been successful.

Another way of approaching the situation is to respond to the words spoken.

Skill of paraphrasing and reflective listening

This skill requires firstly that the teacher listens to the pupil, secondly that they believe in the potential constructive side of the pupil, (Rogers', 1967, core condition of genuineness, and unconditional regard), thirdly that the teacher uses helpful language rather than the roadblocks to communication outlined so powerfully by Gordan (1974).

This means using words and phrases that encourage the pupil to say how they feel, to identify and clarify the problem as they see it and to solve their own problems, avoiding language which orders, commands, directs, warns, threatens, moralises, preaches, advises, lectures, judges, criticises or blames.

A powerfully effective skill here is for the teacher to paraphrase or repeat the student's words:

'So you find this boring?'. The result of such an intervention is usually a further clarification which helps the teacher to get a better perspective whilst at the same time de-escalating a potential conflict.

Checking out an unspoken feeling

One of the skills which can get powerful results in terms of a change in pupil behaviour, is that of checking out an interpretation, or to look for a likely unspoken feeling, such as concern because the task is too hard. In our illustration the teacher may say: 'I'm wondering if what you're actually saying is that there's something you're finding difficult and need some help with.' Unless the teacher habitually checks statements made by children in order to clarify the motive, assumptions will continue to be made, sometimes with negative results.

Stating your own feelings

This is the skill that most of the teachers we work with initially find most threatening.

They often think that if they tell the students how they are feeling right now as a result of the students' behaviour, they will appear vulnerable. The result of trying this technique is that this is not the case. To be persuaded to try, however, teachers usually have to have been convinced of our premise in the former chapter, that the students are behaving this way because they are vulnerable, are hurting, and do not have any other way of expressing their pain.

Once this is accepted, the logic of modelling appropriate behaviour is clear. The appropriate behaviour is to say how you feel instead of acting it out.

Again the effect of saying how you feel, without apportioning blame, is almost always one of de-escalation. It is vital however that teachers say how they feel *as a result of* the pupils' behaviour, and do not say: 'You *make* me feel.'

Some examples of the way this has been used successfully in discipline situations is outlined by Gordan (1974) and Hall and Hall (1988).

Ability to use new scripts

The authors of this book have come to realise that teaching new language patterns is essential. In this book these are referred to as 'scripts', and are discussed more fully in the chapters on dealing with disputes. They have found through their own action research in the classroom that in order to effectively change the behaviour of the pupil with emotional and behavioural difficulties it is important to address the wider language needs of the whole class.

The explanation for the success in behavioural terms of addressing script formation for all the pupils in the class, lies in theory of self-esteem. The language in the classroom affects the environment and ethos, the quality of feedback and the relationships between pupils and the teacher.

Learning and using new scripts is a very difficult skill. Old scripts really do die hard. When emotions are aroused, they jog the script memory and before you know it you have trotted out the same words and phrases that you hated your own mother or father or teacher using to you. (A useful book on scripts and their inheritance is *Born to Win* by James and Jongeward, 1971).

Learning new scripts is very powerful because it challenges pupils with behavioural problems. After all, they are locked into the unsuccessful old script just as much as the teacher.

One aspect of scripts which needs to be learned is the modulation of voice tone to be non-aggressive and non-threatening. This too helps in building up a trusting and positive relationship. Combining this with non-threatening language and the skill to listen attentively to both what is said and the feelings and meaning behind the words can have almost instant effects on difficult children.

When teachers model the effectiveness of using such skills, particularly new scripts for dealing with disputes, then the peer group can also be taught to use them with dramatic effect.

One such script is the three part message which is drawn from the work of Thomas Gordan (1974), who suggests:

— a description of the behaviour the pupil has exhibited;
— a statement of the teacher's feelings;
— and a statement about the consequences for the teacher of the pupil's behaviour.

A three part message response to the illustration might be: 'When you say "It's boring" Daniel, I feel hurt, it's as though all my efforts to prepare an interesting lesson for all of you have been a waste of time. If so I would like you to say that, in the way that we all practised in class yesterday when we were learning how to ask for help.'

To enable teachers to make these kinds of interventions when student feelings are running very high, this kind of response has to be practised over and again by the teacher in lower key situations. So that when an incident happens on a Friday afternoon that would fill anyone with an intense irrational anger, the response is constructive and not a shout.

Giving feedback

Whilst we recognise that teachers are giving children feedback all the time, we also see that the skill to give good quality teacher feedback is rare. Good quality does not mean positive feedback alone, but the information given to the child should be accurate and specific. This is far better than referring globally to the person or their ability and can be supportive of children's self-esteem whilst helping to eradicate unwanted behaviours. Negative feedback for bad behaviour should be balanced with positive feedback for good. The best language for feedback is 'non-blaming' as recommended above. Peer group feedback can be helpful and needs to be structured to ensure that it is supportive rather than destructive of the teacher's aims to eradicate bad behaviour.

In line with the evidence from self-esteem theory outlined in the previous chapter we believe that feedback, its amount and quality, is an aspect of teacher behaviour which can influence children with emotional and behavioural difficulties.

Ability to empathise

Empathy is not a feeling, it is a skill. It is different from sympathy because it requires that you place yourself in the shoes of the other person, you see the world through their eyes and experience the world through their feelings, which means you will feel their pain. (Egan, 1975; Rogers, 1951; Munro *et al*, 1979). The skill involved is of training yourself to ask the question, 'How would I be feeling in that situation?' and then checking out with the pupil whether that is indeed how they are feeling. Initially you may not always be right, but the system of questioning yourself and then checking with them will make you a person who is skilled in empathising.

Teachers who are empathetic can recognise what is going on because they have trained themselves to remember incidents in their lives when they behaved in the same way as the pupil. Their skill is to work out from their remembered experience what the child might be thinking and feeling, to check these feelings out with the pupil and work out what strategies might help.

The amount of work that the teacher has to do to understand the student in order to help them learn to their potential then becomes apparent. Teachers cannot possibly know how it feels to be working class and struggling at school, because the very fact that they have become teachers means that it is almost bound to be outside their personal experience. In the same way they cannot know how it feels to be black if they are white or female if they are male. What they can do is to come to an approximation of how it might feel to be that person through empathetic listening.

Rather than seeing socio-economic class as a reason for protecting and excusing students from participating fully and being successful in the National Curriculum, teachers should be seeing social class as an area of lack of direct personal experience, an indicator that teachers have to work harder, listen harder to understand what it is students are really saying, and try to imagine how they as teachers might feel if they were in the actual circumstances of different individuals in their class.

A teacher who is able to empathise will be one who uses information about a child's background as a tool for understanding some of the motives behind the behaviour, whilst recognising that the actual behaviour takes place in the classroom. The teacher might well have been one of the people involved in the incident and so the behaviour may feel directed at them. Empathy enables them to stand back from that situation and realise that they personally are not the target but their role might be. One phenomenon that often occurs is that students act out the feelings of anger, frustration and unfairness that they experience as a result of a poor relationship with another teacher when they are with the one with whom they feel safe. This has been recognised in the special school milieus which have taken a psycho-dynamic approach to pupils with emotional and behavioural difficulties. For an overview of the history and thinking behind such institutions, see Cooper, Smith and Upton, 1993.

Teachers have expressed to us their anxiety that their perceived lack of specialist expertise may cause them to damage rather than help children. Skills training has helped them to realise that empathy is a skill which is achievable for them and has powerful therapeutic effects for the child. This is not to say that the child should not have counselling when appropriate but that teachers can learn some of the skills of counselling and use them as well. After all, the teacher is usually the first one on the scene and so can make a difference.

CHAPTER 3

Classroom Environment

Separate or integrated provision

Need for a therapeutic environment

The 1981 Education Act outlined the way in which pupils' individual needs could be identified and met with appropriate provision both in mainstream and special schools. Initially the main focus of the integration debate was on the question of how pupils with physical differences could be accommodated and educated in mainstream schools. Over the last decade, as a result of some innovative and sensitive work, provision is increasingly being made possible within the mainstream. Resourcing for support teachers, on site units, adaptations of buildings and specialised equipment have all contributed to the success of integrating special needs.

However, as Fish (1989) and the Audit Commission (1992) have noted, the one group of special needs that is increasingly provided for in a separate environment is the group with emotional and behavioural difficulties.

The authors recognise that damaged children need a therapeutic environment. Historically this kind of environment has been provided in small groups, either in mainstream or in special schools which allowed teachers to form close relationships and where approaches based on psycho-dynamic psychology could be used. The fundamental basis of this is the cathartic effects of the safe expression of feelings. In order to allow time for this therapy the curriculum was sometimes minimal and with many low expectations of academic success (Cooper, Smith and Upton, 1994).

The resource implication of the therapeutic environment is that only a few of the children at the extreme end of the continuum can be placed in the special therapeutic environment. This is why teachers in mainstream place such great store by the placement of youngsters with emotional and behavioural difficulties in segregated settings and why it is seen for many as the end of the statementing process.

As indicated earlier, the reported experience of our teachers is that as soon as they remove the main disrupter another one starts to take on that role. This would indicate that it cannot be solely a within-child problem and that removal to a specialist environment is ineffective. For us the concept of a continuum indicates that all the students can behave in challenging ways. It is just that they usually leave it to the other more vulnerable students to act it out. If such vulnerable students end up being expelled, they will often talk about being 'set up' by other students, and that they found it difficult to escape from a pattern of behaviour and expectations. For them the 'new start' offered by the expulsion does have a positive angle, although clearly the damage to the self-esteem in terms of 'failure' and being 'not wanted' that expulsion brings, would indicate that earlier intervention work to help the child break the pattern is preferable.

When one of these 'others' are removed, or when curriculum arrangements lead to a smaller group setting, then teachers can often be heard to comment in consternation about the cheeky and difficult behaviour of children whom they had previously viewed as 'good' rather than 'naughty', or co-operative rather than difficult. This is one of the reasons that teachers think that they cannot give responsibility to pupils.

It is our view that the principle of a therapeutic community is a good one. However it is also our view that it is not good for students who are already damaged to be sent away under a cloak of punishment, which is the inevitable experience of those who go down the statementing route to special schools over behaviour difficulties.
This is partly because:

- circumstances in the environment that have given rise to the child behaving in that way have not had to change, so are likely to create other children who behave in that way;

- children act out on behalf of others in the group; that is, they carry the feelings of dissatisfaction and disruption that all the others are feeling to some extent, and which the other members of the group project onto them;

- there are just not ever going to be enough places to meet the need. It is emotional and behavioural difficulties that teachers find most difficult to handle and therefore that get the highest number of referrals for statementing;

- it is not good for students to be separated from their peers. Although the therapeutic environment can provide both a respite from other children and from the home and the school, and can meet their needs for a place that is safe, secure and permanent (Wills, 1960), there is a problem about reintegration and children coping when they come out of that respite situation into society at large. Research shows (Lund, 1987, and Lewis, 1971) that there is evidence of the pupil's self-esteem dropping at the point of reintegration indicating that the effects of raising the self-esteem in the therapeutic setting do not transfer. The reason that the reintegration is always going to be difficult is that the pupils and teachers in mainstream are no more skilled to deal with the re-integrated child than they were when he/she was removed. Nothing will have changed in terms of classroom ethos and delivery.

Special needs as a continuum

The 1981 Education Act enshrined in legislation the powerful argument that every child is an individual. The statementing process seeks to meet

28

an individual child's needs by examining the problem and resourcing the provision that will alleviate the difficulty. The 1994 D.F.E. document *Pupils with Problems* provides a useful overview of the expectations of schools before statementing and the resultant extra resources likely to be considered. The 1994 document contains a section on the 'staged approach', in which it stresses the importance of observation and of raising pupils' self-esteem. The authors concur with these recommendations, and seek to provide practical ways of enabling classroom teachers to improve their preventative, school based approaches at stages one to three.

The authors of this book are in agreement with the notion of a continuum of special needs as outlined in the 1981 Act and reiterated in the 1993 Code of Practice, and also with the notion of a continuum of emotional and behavioural difficulties (D.F.E. 1993). However, we also take the view that the students who are usually identified by teachers as having emotional and behavioural difficulties are simply the tip of the iceberg. These children are the ones who act out their feelings in a noticeable way. It is our experience that underneath the tip is a mountain of other pupils who also have emotional difficulties but, because they do not present with the same intensity, they do not get identified.

In this sense we argue that everything we recommend for the student with emotional and behavioural difficulties is appropriate for all students. The reverse is also true, everything that is done for students without emotional and behavioural difficulties needs to be appropriate for whole class teaching. We take the view that good practice in the area of special educational needs is good classroom practice, and offer some suggestions for the answer to the question, 'What is good classroom practice?'

The authors of this book argue that if the emotional and social selves of the students are ignored, then the poor behaviour and/or poor work output, which are symptoms of 'things not being right' so far as the child's emotional state is concerned will interfere with the amount of progress made on the syllabus. It is our collective experience that bringing the emotional and social behaviours out into the open curriculum, and dealing with them as part of the lesson, not only increases on-task behaviour in the long term, but also leads to an increase in motivation, personal responsibility, group responsibility and quality of work produced.

Creating a therapeutic environment in the mainstream

The view that is presented in this book is that we need to train teachers to be able to deliver the curriculum in an environment which includes elements of therapy. That is:

– expression of feelings, close relationships, skills for dealing with disputes, skills of empathy and so on…

Teachers need to create classrooms which echo the Wills criteria of safe, secure, permanent and mine. This means that the normal sanction of exclusion from the classroom needs to be at a minimum, questioned and (ideally) stopped.

This is because children with emotional and behavioural difficulties cannot have their need for security met with the threat of exclusion from the classroom hanging over them. We recognise that there will probably always need to be a special unit for some children. However, the problem with the present provision is that it is inevitably associated with punishment. Children feel that they have failed in their mainstream setting because of the feedback from teachers. A more constructive alternative would be one where the mainstream classroom was so similar in environment to the segregated setting that there would be no problem in transfer from one setting to another. Additionally the segregated setting would be a place chosen by the child for temporary respite and extra help. Some schools are actually doing some of this in the way that they have encouraged children to ask for time out, and have set up time out rooms. This is not the same thing as the teacher sending them out, it is working towards independence and self control in the child.

The creation of such an environment in ordinary mainstream classrooms is more likely to help children who have behavioural difficulties through accident and circumstance and medical reasons, as well as achieving the aims outlined in the D.F.E. 1994 document on discipline: i.e. to create students who have a clear sense of right and wrong, who are self-disciplined and have a respect for others.

We know that just telling students that they are doing wrong does not work. What is needed is a programme that teaches the students the skills they need to get it right.

We believe that it is possible to teach the curriculum through the therapeutic exercises outlined in this book. This benefits all of the children and meets the emotional needs of them all. What we describe is a preventative approach so there are likely to be fewer discipline problems, learning difficulties, referrals, or need for expensive resources.

Personal responsibility – teacher and child

Sharing power for teachers means handing over power and responsibility to the pupils and this, for many teachers, is quite threatening. When faced with a very disruptive pupil, the wish to retain power is understandably immense. The wish to protect the other pupils is often paramount in the mind of the teacher, and rightly so. However, the constant battle to retain a power position is the one which most exhausts the teacher and is one which they are ultimately destined never to win. By handing over some of that power and responsibility, the struggle ceases. It is our experience that the power is then awarded back to the teacher, with the pupils' consensus.

This can be done through changes in organisation of the classroom structures, the use of co-operative groups, negotiation of the rules and changes in curriculum delivery, particularly from written to oral input and outcomes. These strategies are fully outlined throughout this book and in *Teaching Special Needs* (McNamara and Moreton, 1993). They have been found to achieve great success for all pupils and have particularly good results for children with emotional and behavioural difficulties. This shift in power changes the classroom ethos quite dramatically. We have found that other outcomes follow quickly. The level of pupil on-task behaviour increases and the motivation and quality of work also soars. Teacher talk interestingly falls at the same time. Teachers have reported that they actually have time to teach.

The first step in adopting the approach recommended in this book is that of the teacher asserting their own responsibility for students with special educational needs, especially those with emotional and behavioural difficulties. This will mean a different way of working with other adults in the classroom – a move away from seeing them as experts towards a partnership approach.

The reliance on the expert

It is often perceived by teachers and school management that in order to deal with the external problems which they see as causing problems for pupils with emotional and behavioural difficulties, experts are needed. These experts come from a variety of professional backgrounds and include doctors, educational psychologists, social workers and other medical therapists.

It is our view that reliance on external sources of help tends to increase the problem rather than solve it. (Galloway and Goodwin, 1987; Tattum, 1982, 1986.) This is because it sets up a dependency syndrome whereby teachers come to expect that the responsibility for such students lies with others, such as special needs support personnel. Cooper *et al* (1994) note that the arrival of the specialist teacher in the classroom may well result in a de-skilling of the class teacher.

This is because the hidden curricular message to the classroom teacher is that they lack the right skills to deal with this child whilst the special teacher possesses them. Since someone else is taking responsibility for this child there is little motivation for the class teacher to acquire the skills. In addition, since the specialist teacher is working on a one-to-one basis with the child, the conclusion for the class teacher is that they cannot do what the specialist is doing in a class of thirty. Again there would be little point in learning the skills since the class teacher needs to work with the whole class. The result is a de-motivated teacher and confirmation of the belief that this child needs withdrawing for small group and one-to-one work.

The child meanwhile may relish the relationship with the specialist teacher but at the same time they inevitably have their sense of failure confirmed. Clearly there must be something wrong with them because nothing has changed in the classroom and they have been singled out for special help. In particular, nothing has changed in terms of their relationship with the other children or with the teacher. In fact the specialist teacher has to hope that they alone can raise this child's self-esteem. As noted earlier this is unlikely without the co-operation of the peer group.

It is a concern of the authors that the staged identification process of the code of practice (1994) will perhaps encourage teachers to label pupils earlier than they would have before. This may mean that in addition to being labelled, assessed and singled out for specialist help which may not fit well with their self-esteem, such students may also vent their negative feelings on the group that is just a bit worse than themselves, those who are further along in the identification process.

This behaviour has already been observed by the author during one statementing process, when so many outside agency representatives came in and observed, interviewed and made reports on the child that the result was aggression by the observed child (who was being statemented), towards younger children, and a sister in particular.

Our view is that there is a causal relationship between the classroom environment and the behaviour of the pupil. In which case there is little point in focusing on the behaviour and emotions of the pupil unless the teacher is prepared to make changes in the classroom environment as well, especially in terms of the relationships between the pupil and its peers and the pupil with the teacher. It is our belief that the child is too damaged to initiate the changes in both behaviour and relationships, therefore the onus must be on the teacher to make those changes. It is our experience that when teachers do start to make these changes then the pupil starts to change too. In classrooms where the ethos has changed in the direction indicated in this chapter, the class teacher and specialist work together in close harmony with interchanging roles, and all the pupils in the class vie for help from both of them, as well as helping each other.

Ethos

As has been observed above, social class being seen as a deficit model has often led to a teaching style that becomes ever more didactic with the 'low-ness' of the social class. This is best summed up by the reported statements from many teachers, 'Well you might be able to do that with middle class children but our children need structure.' The assumption is that the students know nothing and they have no experiences that are of any relevance to school.

For example we have often been told by teachers of French or English as a second language that they can't do pair work because the pupils have not got the language to talk to each other, they have only got the language that the teacher has taught them. Our own experience of using French in France is that this is patently not the case, and that the imperative to communicate results in all kinds of learning that the teacher could not have predicted. Hence the emphasis on communicative language teaching styles.

In fact our research has shown that when students are asked to brainstorm using their own forms of expressive language prior to a topic being taught (see McNamara and Moreton, 1993) then a wealth of prior knowledge and understanding in that topic area is apparent, as well as a different and varied set of experiences that the teacher may not have even thought of. The consequence of viewing pupils who exhibit challenging behaviour as needing structure is that they tend to be kept on a 'tight rein', given lots of worksheets to do and hence have had little practice at group work or relationship formation in the classroom. It is our view that it is these very pupils who can benefit most from oral work, drama, simulation, group work and role play approaches to the curriculum, but that in order to do so they must first be taught the skills they will need to function effectively in groups in a structured way. In this sense we agree that 'these children need structure' but it is a structured approach to the skills they need for working independently, co-operatively and responsibly that we identify.

As indicated in the Elton report, 1989, there are a variety of aspects to creating a classroom ethos. In this context we are referring to the hidden curriculum that says, 'This is how we do it in this classroom'. The organisation, the teacher's style, the curriculum content and delivery can all influence the way a classroom feels.

Classroom organisation

The way that classroom ethos operates is subtle, and consists of many different rules, few of which are expressed overtly. It affects the noise level, the peer group interactions and the level of teacher stress. The most consistent comment that teachers we work with make is about their anxiety in relation to noise level. Despite all the work on student centred learning through TVE, there is still an attitude amongst managers of schools that silence means learning and noise means an incompetent teacher. Many teachers will say things like, 'Well I'd love to try out your oral based activities with my students, but my classroom is right beside the entrance and the Head Teacher's office...'

If this is the case we recommend whole staff discussions about teaching and learning styles, ethos, and hidden curricula messages, with teachers being prepared to be assertive and say what they really think about the intimidation they sometimes feel from their managers which is detrimental to the appropriate teaching and learning environment for their students.

Organisation of furniture and fittings can also effect the classroom ethos. Having rows of desks with the teacher in a powerful front of the board position gives clear, although maybe hidden, messages about learning. It says that pupils are empty vessels to be filled by a greater knowledge. There are also clear messages about who holds the power and the responsibility for the conduct in the classroom. Even when curriculum delivery is not along these lines the message is still very powerful. There has been a tendency to interpret the recent findings of Professor Alexander (1992) as it being important to return to children being seated in rows. The authors of this book disagree with this conclusion. The authors' experience concurs with the finding in the Oracle Project (Galton *et al*, 1980) where it was rare to find co-operative tasks given to groups when seated at a group table; more often they were given individual tasks.

Our interpretation of Alexander's findings that children in primary schools seated in groups were often off-task, is that there is a need to match seating arrangement with task. That is to say, when children need to work individually at a task, it is helpful if their tables are facing the wall as in the photograph, (page 34). They can then use the open space created for pair work, small group discussions or whole circle work. These activities show how a variety of seating can provide for a variety of tasks.

In secondary schools a similar approach can be taken and students can be trained to move the furniture to this position if there is a conflict over room usage.

Teacher's style

Teacher's style is one aspect which is bound to have an effect on the general classroom ethos experienced by all the pupils. A teacher who constantly shouts at all the children is likely to engender an atmosphere of fear and remoteness in relationships. As previously suggested, the emotionally and behaviourally disturbed child may well be expressing the thoughts and feelings of the other children in the class. Shouting is often the way in which children try to assert their power and we can see that this is a lesson they have learnt from the adults and teachers in their prior experience. Teachers who gain and hold onto classroom power through verbal aggression are likely, through modelling that behaviour, to have it turned on them by some pupils.

The authors of this book recognise that shouting with sheer frustration when faced with very difficult pupils is understandable. What we wish to demonstrate are strategies which reduce the frustration and stress for the teacher so that they can model, and indeed enjoy, a different way of operating.

The relationship that pupils have with their teacher is crucial for the way in which they behave in the classroom. On the most basic level, children will try to succeed with their behaviour or their work for a teacher they feel comfortable with and whom they like. Their motivation to try will be lacking if they do not feel good about their relationship with their teacher. A quick survey in the staff room will usually show a high correlation between preferred teaching subject and the remembered relationship that teacher had with their own subject teacher as a pupil. The type of relationship, open, trusting and positive or closed, mistrusting and negative is clearly important. The closer the relationship the teacher and child forms the more likely it is to encourage self disclosure, which in its turn influences the amount of trust. (Egan, 1975; Rogers, 1951; Jourard, 1971; Hamblin, 1974, 1989). When there is a positive relationship then the child can trust enough to take risks. This might be to try out a new way of behaving, or it might be the preparedness to seek help and advice when faced with learning problems. The way in which the teacher behaves in terms of their relationship to the pupil can, therefore, have a very powerful effect on children's behaviour.

Curriculum delivery

Delivery which might be considered 'good practice' can give hidden messages to pupils which may affect their view of themselves and their behaviour. Accepted practice needs to be examined when thinking about a child who has emotional and behavioural difficulties. Practices which may be useful for other

pupils might be very destructive for these pupils. It might be that, on reflection, teachers find that the good practice is in fact only good for a very few.

One such instance that can be more closely examined is that of differentiated worksheets. These may take a great deal of time to prepare but prove to be ineffective because of the children's awareness of who is doing the hardest and who the easiest sheets. This is clear feedback on academic expectations. If you, the child, are always given the easy sheet there is little incentive to do anything else. If it is too easy then you can 'struggle' to ensure that you remain having very little to do, a low expectation with a low output. If it is so easy it is boring then you have plenty of time to amuse yourself by behaving badly, annoying others, disrupting the teacher, and still complete the work.

The importance of oracy, skills training and structures

Bernstein talked about a restricted code in language for studentsfrom a low socio-economic class background. In contrast, the authors' experience has brought them to the conclusion that having a restricted code for dealing with disputes is not just characteristic of pupils from a low economic class but is also present in those from other class backgrounds. Teachers need to teach all the students in the class the language of negotiation so that they have choices in the language that they can use. This also gives them the skills tokeep to the rules which say no verbal abuse, no answering back, no violence, no swearing.

Our recommendation is that all pupils need to learn the language for: stating their own feelings, showing empathy, negotiation skills including giving feedback; friendship skills; which include: encouraging others, helping others, peer tutoring,

The way in which we think each skill should be taught follows the formula below:

- model the skills in action;
- teach the skills;
- provide opportunities for practising the skills;
- praise and use positive feedback when the skills are used.

Prerequisite skills

There are some speaking and listening skills that are necessary prerequisites before pupils can embark on the strategies outlined in the following chapters. With some pupils it may be necessary to start right back at the beginning of a skills training programme which teaches the students how to use the correct non-verbal skills for listening attentively to each other. This can be a useful way of dealing with disputes that begin, 'He looked at me funny.' Included below are some aspects of these prerequisite skills. With students where there are large numbers with emotional and behavioural difficulties, it may take some time to simply teach them these skills, typically with Year 6 pupils it takes about six months to teach them the skills they need to be able to work together in groups, in order to do the first Rule Making Exercise. In secondary schools therefore it may take even longer because of the number of different teachers they have. In our experience the younger the pupils are when we start this kind of work, the quicker it is to teach the prerequisite skills; this may be an indication of the learning for 'dependence' and 'aggression' that is a consequence of the more 'normal', tight rein approach. It is however essential that the pupils have got the prerequisite skills before they go on to the harder main skills.

The role of the teacher in teaching the prerequisite skills is to:

- provide a model of changed scripts;
- help the pupils to be at ease with talk in the classroom, and learn good listening skills, which allow them to attend to what is actually being said, not what they assume is being said;
- allow them to be comfortable with sharing how they see something with one other peer group member;
- allow them to become comfortable sharing with more than one other peer group member;
- help them to become used to hearing what it is that they have just said by hearing it repeated back by another peer group member;
- help the students to practice observing what actually happens and listen accurately to what is said;
- help the pupils to feedback their observations;
- help the pupils to check out feelings behind observed behaviours.

Main skills

The aims of the skills training programme as outlined in this book are for the teacher to:

- help the pupils to observe various scripts in action;
- help the pupils to try out new scripts in role plays provided by the teacher;
- help the pupils to try out new scripts in situations devised by the participants;
- help the pupils to try out new scripts in real situations.

This small steps approach is imperative for students who are locked into negative behaviours. Unless the prerequisite skills are taught then the teaching of new scripts will prove too difficult and fail to help the children.

In order to teach the prerequisite skills a number of particular structures are recommended. Below are a series of activities which illustrate these structures. They can be used with a wide variety of sizes of groups, different age and ability groups and the subject content altered to enable them to be used many times. The skill of adaptation of these activities is one which we have found all teachers who use our methodology soon find very easy. This follows a small steps approach beginning with basic skills.

The authors are convinced that making pupils of all ages work in random pairs is vitally important. In fact our experiences show that if teachers do not use random pairs then the rest of the strategies outlined in this book will be greatly reduced in their effectiveness. The reasons are well documented in research evidence linked to self-esteem and interpersonal skills. (Burns, 1982, provides a good overview of this).

If pupils are left to work in friendship pairs, then what happens is that the ones who are similarly 'attractive', which in our culture means those with an athletic looking body and no physical defects, gravitate towards each other. The others sort themselves out and end up in pairs of similar levels of 'unattractiveness'. Teachers will remember the horrors of being 'picked' for sports teams – this process goes on at a subtle level in the early days of group formation. If nothing else is done by the teacher to intervene then the pupils will continue to view the others outside of their own 'safe' group of four or six youngsters with a mix of hostility, suspicion and fear. If, on the other hand the teacher succeeds in 'mixing the group' then pupils come to know the person behind both the physical appearance and the reputation. Since, as noted in the chapters above, there is stereotyping going on by both the teachers (who affect the pupils' perceptions of one another) and the students themselves, the chances of pupils maintaining very negative views about students who are different to themselves in terms of: colour of skin, social class, way of dressing, gender, ethnic group, and special need, for example, is very high indeed.

Friendship pairs also mean that invariably the difficult children end up without a chosen partner and so are put together where they have no good model to follow and are likely to fail and so disrupt everyone else. The use of random pairs as a structure ensures that the pupils both work with as many different members of the class as possible and also get to know the person behind the stereotype. It also takes away some of the anger some pupils feel if they are made to work with someone of the teacher's choosing.

For those pupils who behave badly there will be the opportunity for others to get beyond their impression of a 'bad' person for a short time in a safe environment. For those who find it difficult to work with others the pair is the easiest place to try out different ways of behaving. The pupils are likely to resist this way of working initially because it is new for them, especially the older ones. We suggest here several strategies:

- A clear explanation to the students as to why you want them to work in random pairs and not friendship pairs – it is helpful if you can give them some observation feedback that illustrates the limited circles of pupils with whom they have contact. Explanations which include a reference to the ability to 'work' with others in the world of work, that we are trying to create a classroom of colleagues not friends, just as the teachers in schools form staff rooms of colleagues, where they may not socialise with each other, they may not even like each other very much, but they can all work with each other.

- A clear statement about the fact that boys and girls working together does not mean that any one thinks they are girlfriend and boyfriend and any teasing in that direction is juvenile and will be given teacher disapproval

- Teacher insistence that this is how we do things in this class, and a consistent use of it in small doses.
- The use of same gender pairings then mixed gender fours if there are strong cultural taboos about eye contact and close proximity with members of the opposite gender.
- Teacher approval when students are working well together – peer feedback to support this in the shape of listening spotter sheets can help – see chapter seven on dispute management.

Once the use of random pairs is clearly established as part of the normal classroom routine many pupils will help to devise interesting curriculum related cards, pictures, symbols, and other methods of getting class members organised.

Pair work for oracy

There are a wide variety of activities that will teach and then remind children of the need for careful, accurate listening to what is being said. We begin with talking in pairs, as this is a very safe environment in which children might begin to risk behaving differently to the 'normal' class role. Pair talk is important for children with emotional and behavioural problems for a number of reasons.

Pair work for reducing attention seeking behaviour

Firstly it is helpful for ensuring that children listen carefully. It also gives them positive feedback that they are being listened to. For children with behavioural difficulties this feeling of being given someone's full attention has clear benefits. Many 'popular' but disruptive pupils owe their popularity to their acting out rather than to real friendships within the class. Much attention seeking and disruptive behaviour occurs because the pupils feel that no one is taking any notice of them. By behaving badly they gain the teacher's attention and the acclaim of their peers. If they receive attention through a 'pairs talking and listening' activity on a regular basis then their need to get attention by acting out is reduced.

All pupils need to be taught how to sit opposite to one another, to give appropriate eye contact and to paraphrase. Ideas for this are outlined more fully in McNamara and Moreton, 1993. The more able they are socially the less time this will take. The exchange of roles from speaker to listener is particularly helpful for the pupil with emotional and behavioural difficulties, as they are in desperate need of a range of roles to play instead of their current one.

Many teachers of disruptive pupils have been sceptical of this view but on trying it out have found a real reduction in pupils' attention seeking, particularly in talking out of turn. Perhaps this can be attributed to the fulfilling of a need to talk, particularly about oneself. With pupils being given so little of the talking time in the school day the frustration for some children, who may be used to talking constantly at home, might come from bottling up what they want to say and having to wait their turn. Talking in pairs can alleviate this frustration. The work on oracy over the last few years confirms earlier research findings which show that teacher talk dominates the classroom. (Flanders, 1970; Tough, 1976, 1977, 1979; Wilkinson, 1965; Norman, 1990).

Pair work to reduce talking out of turn

A further benefit comes from changing the nature of talk within the classroom. Teachers and pupils are used to teachers stopping a great deal of talking. Those children who find it hard not to talk, or talk at the 'wrong' time can easily get labelled as disruptive. By using paired talking in the classroom their natural wish to talk is legitimised and the 'sin' of talking becomes their 'talent'. For constant talkers out of turn this new emphasis allows them to reassess their self image and see the positive benefits of verbally expressing oneself, rather than merely dealing with the negative aspects of not knowing the 'curriculum knowledge' or not being allowed to talk.

Paired talking also allows the teacher to give these children practice in starting and stopping conversations in a very structured way. For those who have a history of talking when the teacher is waiting this is particularly helpful as it gives them an opportunity to be different. There are many signalling devices for stopping the talk in pairs that can be used.

One that is used by the authors with primary aged children is for the teacher to raise their hand. As soon as anyone sees the raised hand they stop talking and raise their hand too. The wave of raised hands has an accompanying fall in the level of talk and very soon those who have not stopped are left 'high and dry' talking alone. The peer pressure to stop is enormously effective, even on hardened cases. They key here is that it is not the teacher waiting for them, but the children with their sea of raised hands. When it is silent the teacher lowering their hand is the signal that they do so too and await the next instruction. With secondary students and teachers a gentle shush noise or cards held like football signals, with red for stop, green for go, are successful.

3.1 All pupils need to be taught to sit opposite each other

Finally, many behavioural problems are linked with the academic failures that students have experienced in school. Whether the failure produced the poor behaviour or the poor behaviour produced the failure does not matter. What any intervention needs to ensure is that both aspects are tackled. Paired talking has the advantage that it gives a good behaviour model, structured, with rules and policed by the peer group, whilst giving an opportunity for success academically.

This academic success is linked to the verbalisation of concepts with the stress away from the written text. Pair work can be an alternative start to any subject lesson, rather than the more common pattern of a question and answer session with the whole group, to review or recall previous learning. This could be of benefit to many pupils (including those with emotional and behavioural difficulties) who sometimes find it difficult to re-orientate themselves to the content after a break in time. This could also help those children who are, for whatever reason, frequently absent or late. Paired talking to recall prior learning is also helpful in preparing the students for the next step in their learning. It helps to get them up to date but it also allows them to verbally check out their understanding before moving on. Verbalising your understanding is a very important part of the learning process. Any teacher will know that when you try to explain something to someone you have a better understanding of it yourself. (Vygotsky, 1962, 1978; Mercer, 1991).

This verbalising provides another important opportunity, and that is for students to check out their understanding of specialist words by using their own more common language to express the same ideas. As students get older there is an expectation that they will use the 'proper' words but these are not always the most helpful in actually grasping the concept. It is clear that pupils learn from each other when talking about and explaining their work in this way. This is what we mean by differentiation by outcome, rather than task.

3.2 Pair work removing the stress of the written text

What has often been lacking for many children is the structure within the classroom to talk specifically about the concepts they are exploring. Just putting children together and allowing talk does not achieve this, to the frustration of many teachers. It just creates a noise! By indicating the value you place on talking together about the concept and by giving regular opportunities to do it then you give great opportunities for increased success to many of our most difficult pupils.

When a curriculum relies very heavily on written text, notes and written answers then the failed reader or poor writer not only feels a failure, but is bound to be a failure. These academic failures then go on to produce many of our behavioural problems. By systematically beginning every lesson with paired talking these children have a more positive view of their prior learning and so a more positive chance to learn though that lesson. The more talk structures that can be introduced throughout the lesson the better, particularly for pupils with emotional and behavioural difficulties.

Rules for circle work

The main rule to establish here is that the pupils sit so that they can see all the others in the group, this means a true circle and not a sausage, and they let others speak, so they take it in turns to speak. They usually need structured help with this, using both speaking devices such as a 'conch' – a pencil or board rubber, only the one holding it can speak, and going round the group with each saying something, no 'pass' allowed, only 'thinking time' which means we will come back to you. It is also helpful to have stem statements to complete: 'my favourite food is…' and to begin with sharing information about 'me'.

Rules for brainstorming

Brainstorming means that everyones' ideas are valued, the best way to achieve this is to give groups one piece of paper but either as many pens as there are members of the group, or strict instructions that the 'scribe' will need to only write down that which is said, not the scribe's interpretation or summary of what has been said. Prioritising and categorisation are the next steps after brainstorm.

Teaching pupils to work in small groups

How many of us have complained that children cannot work together? How often is it that a child can work when isolated and not disrupt but when working with any other children immediately disturbs their work and does none of his own? For many children the solution has been either further isolation, a desk alone or sitting near the teacher, or withdrawal in a small group with a teacher's more constant supervision. We justify this by saying that they need more adult attention. This however does not fit with the reality. What they need is to be able to work with other children without adult supervision.

It seems to us that the reason many children have behavioural problems is that they don't know how to work with others. They lack the social skills to deal with that small peer group when an academic task is at hand. This might be due to past academic failure which makes them nervous about being shown up. This is particularly the case when children who relate in the playground or after school hours fail to be able to work together. In many cases however it can be due to the failure of any good model of relating to peers in any situation. Experience of being with other children may be of being bullied, of being 'put down' or laughed at. It may just be an experience of being different. These children are the loners, some of whom might strive to join the others but do so with so little skill that their positive advances are constantly rejected.

The teacher needs to look at both these aspects. Firstly the academic nature of many of the group tasks we present to children. If pupils are failing academically then this will probably appear to them as the worst kind of ordeal, involving them in very public failure. Other children may well emphasise this by openly expressing a reluctance to have this particular child in their group. It is therefore very important when dealing with all children, but particularly those who find it difficult to behave appropriately in a small group, to introduce work in fours in a context which is clearly non-academic. That means it should involve no writing (or only the briefest of recording), be as physical as possible, be verbal, and use creative skills rather than logical thinking. Only when fours work is established should the teacher introduce academic or problem solving activities. Even then, the tasks should remain simple, and all tasks be well below the standard you would expect of the students when working alone. It is the case that four heads might be better than one, but only when those four heads know how to pool their ideas. Until that time they will be using three quarters of their concentration on just being together in a group so only one quarter will be available to the academic task.

Small group skills

Group skills do not just happen. They need to be taught and practised. With many children and adults these may be learned in basic form through socialising with others in a positive environment. If, however, you are dealing with students who have already failed to learn these skills, it is even more important that they are taught very systematically. This systematic teaching of group skills will benefit the children with behavioural problems but will also be of immense benefit to those children who do not appear to present too many problems. These students also lack the more advanced group skills and as they acquire greater levels of understanding of group work, they are better able to deal themselves with those children who still find it difficult.

The reason we advocate using the pairs into fours strategy is to give support from a peer partner to students when first encountering a group of four. This structure is very important because it ensures that the group is initially two pairs meeting, but still working as pairs. The peer partner lends moral support as well as being a person with whom to consult prior to going into the four. This also gives a shared experience and if any failure is experienced the blame is not so personal.

Part of the pairs into fours strategy is to give the same very rigid rule structure to the group, ensuring that the experience is not a free for all. Each person has a specific part of the task and a clear time at which to speak and take their turn. Any roles such as scribe are either rotated or given randomly through a mark on the selection cards so that there is no choosing of leaders or spokespersons etc. The reason for this is twofold. Firstly, it means that no one is rejected as not being able to fulfil a role. Secondly, it ensures that, over time, everyone has a chance to take on unaccustomed roles. As students see each other try out new roles they begin to see that the 'bad' child has talents that they were not previously aware of. This is vitally important for the self-esteem of the child who has been displaying poor behaviour.

Rules for working in fours

Even when the pupils are used to the pair work it is useful to remind them of the rules for working in fours. It may be helpful to have these posted up somewhere.

- Firstly, everyone must have the opportunity to be heard. Banning interruptions and only allowing questions when a person has finished speaking may sound idealistic but is a sound ground rule to establish and children get better at it if you insist.
- Secondly, turn taking is essential if the exercise is not to disintegrate, so encourage the children to decide on order of turns first. Remind them before they start that they need to decide how to take it in turns.
- Thirdly, establish the 'No put down rule'. This means that children are not allowed to say, 'That's a stupid idea' or anything that is destructive, squashing or negative, about someone else's idea. They are allowed to give 'push ups', that is 'That's interesting' or any other positive remarks, praise, or encouragement.
- Fourthly, each person must have the opportunity to speak.
- Fifthly, the personal responsibility rule: it is up to their four to make sure that they all contribute.
- Tell the group that they have between five and ten minutes for sharing these ideas, and it is their job to take responsibility for the time.

Conclusion

The strategies we are outlining in this book reflect our belief that the necessary skills should first be learned by the teacher. These skills must be modelled by the teacher. They should then be specifically taught to the whole class, not just to those children with special needs in this area. As previously explained this is because many of these children are the end of a continuum of behaviour, the tip of the iceberg. It is therefore the case that all the children in the class need to have the skills, both to avoid them taking that child's place and to help each other to behave in the most supportive way to the peer who is having the most difficulty.

	Steps	Teacher Skills	Pupil Skills
Ch 4	Rule formation Boundary setting for security Feeling safe Trusting people you know well All saying the same things	Making rules explicit Feedback skills	Learning to work with one another in pairs and fours Learning to negotiate when the emotional context is low.
Ch 5	Establishing new rules Helping and encouraging Rewarding learning rule keeping behaviour	Praise, reward and encourage Positive feedback skills	Encourage each other Say how you feel when rules are broken Give and receive positive feedback
Ch 6	Identify feelings State feelings Feel feelings	Using different media – drama, art, clay Stating own feelings Using the three part message – describing the behaviour only Checking out with children	Stating own feelings
Ch 7	Being able to see things from someone else's perspective To be able to hear others Teacher learning the rules and skills for managing classroom disputes.	Ability to empathise Broken Record Behaviour description Three part message Hearing two sides No assumptions	Ability to empathise Paraphrasing Listening to others Suspending judgement Starting to trust
Ch 8	Children learning to settle disputes	Role play Structuring steps Continuing to model skills Prompting Giving negative feedback	Broken Record Observing and describing behaviour Using a three part message Negotiation when emotional context is high Giving negative feedback
Ch 9	Learning to help each other	Sharing power and responsibility Creating teaching and responsibility roles Praising for helping skill	Friendship skills Helping skills Peer tutoring skills

Figure 3.3   Skills grid for chapters 4-9

THE GOOD LISTENER

USE YOUR EYES	**DON'T INTERRUPT**
LOOK INTERESTED	**ASK THE RIGHT QUESTIONS**

Figure 3.4 There are lots of ways to be a good listener. Here are four. Draw cartoons to illustrate these skills and add two of your own.

Using a grid for skills training

Stepped approach

In the grid (figure 3.3) provided is an explanation of the layout of this book.

We have identified the prerequisite skills of speaking and listening (figure 3.4) which we have found to be essential before any of the further work for dispute management and appropriate rule keeping behaviour can be embarked upon. In a similar way it is our experience that a stepped approach needs to be taken to reach the target.

That target in our view is a combination of two things:

– pupils who can settle disputes themselves, and

– pupils who can support each other with friendship and help.

For the pupils with emotional and behavioural difficulties they need their peers to be able to do both of these things.

The steps towards this target are the ones outlined in the chapter headings:

rule formation to make pupils feel safe;

learning how to keep the rules;

getting in touch with their own and other people's feelings;

seeing the teacher model good management of arguments or disputes;

with the result that the pupils can learn to do this for themselves.

Using the strategies outside the stepped approach

It would be possible, however, to take some of the strategies in the prerequisites section: random pairs, circlework, introducing the curriculum through brainstorming and pairwork, without the students having high levels of skill. We have found that subjects such as history – for instance the Portuguese explorers, which would otherwise have been daunting and quite boring for some students, take on a different life when presented in the pairs format.

A structure we haven't mentioned in this book – the carousel where pupils sit in a circle in their pairs, and constantly change partners, was used together with brainstorming and poster work (this does not require negotiation, the higher order group work skill), to teach the Portuguese explorers. The students were asked to do a review sheet (figure 3.5) for this work, again a higher order skill although enthusiasm for the day's activities carried many of the weaker, usually more disruptive pupils through this activity.

The pupil comments are to be found in figure 3.6. These pupils are from an inner city estate known in the town as a 'bad estate'. They have been trained by their teacher to start to reflect and some feeling comments can be seen in the work displayed.

Once teachers have acquired the skills outlined in chapter 8 for managing disputes themselves, they will find that even the most daunting groups of pupils can be brought round to do some work at their level. Our experience has taught us that praise for any correct behaviour, 'broken record' instructions, which are

Reviewing Sheet

Think about the lesson and how you feel you have done.
Write honestly. Sign and date your review.

What did I learn?

What was good about this lesson?

What was bad about this lesson?

What did I do well?

What do I need to get better at?

Which other pupil can help me?

Who else can I ask for help?

How do I feel about myself after this lesson? Why?

Date: Signed by:

Figure 3.5   Reviewing Sheet

not derisive, or have any tone in the voice apart from a firm instruction, will get even large groups (one of us worked with a group of 109 pupils in the hall with one other teacher recently), to conform and thank you for their afternoon. In times of one to one conflict between two pupils, clear descriptive statements about your own guess as to the students' feelings are powerful; 'I can see you're angry, it's OK, you don't have to show me how angry you are'.

Whilst many teachers would probably like their pupils to get to the point of chapter nine (learning to settle disputes themselves), and chapter ten (learning to help each other), we would urge caution. These are high order skills that

---

T.

We have talked in a circel and watched a video . I Thought it was O'k and after that we made a Brain Storm I thought that was a bite better than the video after that we made a Group Poster I thought that was very . good and then we had are phote took and I've had a good day the people in my group were grate and I sat next to h. my freind. I tought the work that we did today was better than are normal work and . It was very fun and I though it was much better and I felt happy inside.

H.

I thought yhe video was interesting and good. Talking in a circle was brilliant and it was different than usual . Talking in a double circle was good and you could hear what other people think. Brainstorm was good because you can just put what you think and you would get told what you think. Group poster was good and I knew how I could trust them and be confident with them. When I saw someone taking photos I felt embarassed. Writing about it brings back what happens.

D.

what i did today was wached a video which was about explorer and I thought it was very interesting and I liked it because I learned a lot of new things. Then we taLked in a cirde about what we remembered about the video Iliked listening to other people's views and comments it was fun . Then I talked in a carasel and that was fun as weLl I could talk proparly with most of the people exept Ian I. because he was messing about . then I did a brainstorm where you write your ideas on lots of different pieses of paper and I enjoyed doing this. I liked the Group poster that was great fun I enjoyed this most of aLl my group co-operated briliantly. when the lady came in and took the photographs she took a picture of me and wayne in a carelelle this was another one of my best bits. Now I'm writing about it it seems very boring the other way was better I think .

S.

the video was allrite. And the circle I liked it Talking in a doul circle was qute inteding that was good. Well at forst I all waes said I was the grop ledder But then we sorted it out it then Daniel was the group leddder.

Figure 3.6   Pupil review letters after a day of exercises. Group: T.H.D.S.

most pupils cannot manage, not even very bright pupils, because of the dynamics at work in groups; they will have to go through the previous stages first.

High level skills are very complex

All of the steps and strategies above need to be carried out in an environment where the teacher is modelling behavioural skills and where the students will be taught these skills. This is the content of the second and third columns of the grid (figure 3.3), the teacher behaviour in skills training terms and the pupil behaviour in skills training terms. Consequently the headings for much of the teacher directed information at the beginnings of the chapters which contain references to these skills and the exercises and strategies for the pupils also contain in their headings references to the pupil skills needed.

It is our experience that such a small steps approach to skills training is necessary and that the exercises will not work if teachers try to rush students through the stages or miss out stages. This seems to be because of the complexity of the factors involved in shaping the behaviours the pupils have developed to survive. With such a complexity of factors producing a complex pattern of behaviours that are destructive in their outcome in the long term for the pupil, it is necessary to go right back with the pupil and teach the skills they will need for the next stage of interaction.

We have found that until all this groundwork has been carried out with the peer group, it will not be possible to deal with bullies. Bullying is, in our opinion, an even more deep seated and complex set of factors and behaviours than difficult behaviour. It has enmeshed in it elements of racism which go deep into the psyche of the community. It is only when pupils have let some of their defences drop because they feel supported and valued for who they are, that they will start to hear our feelings about their bullying behaviour.

This approach is different to that traditionally followed by behaviour oriented psychologists, in that it goes back further than the presenting behaviour that is manifesting itself as a problem.

The solution presented in this book is more therapeutic than behaviourist; it is a little like regression therapy but it takes a skills training approach to the regression. To this extent it is rooted very much in the classroom.

It is because of this therapeutic approach that we believe it is necessary to address both teacher and pupil skills. The teacher needs to have a different approach in order to create a therapeutic environment and to give the pupils a good model. From the grid it can be seen that the teacher can either learn to use a new skill at the same time as the pupil, or they can try out and learn their new skills before they teach them to the pupils. When the pupils are working on the strategies outlined in this book they may choose to cut themselves off from what is going on. In bullying work, role play is vital and this will immediately arouse powerful feelings for the bully.

For the specific skills training when you are teaching the pupils to learn the skills for dispute management, our recommendation is that drama is used and that teachers, secondary subject specialists and primary early years through to year 6 teachers, consider booking the hall for this.

This takes time, it is not a 'quick fix'

Sometimes it looks as though some teachers do not like their jobs or children but these are the ones who can be changed by being introduced to teachers who are using the skills successfully.

In this case it is essential that the principles for understanding why you are doing what you are doing are explained and shared. These methods will not work if they are introduced as gimmicks, nor will they work without a fundamental change in emphasis in the power and responsibility – which is why stickers and smiley faces do not work with some teachers and why teachers who use 'listening positions' as a discipline trick will not reap later benefits, nor teachers who castigate talkers by saying, 'You are letting me down'. If teachers gain skills then they start to change their attitudes in the light of the experiences that they have and as a result they start to like children again.

The time it takes for pupils to learn these skills should not be underestimated. If you both teach the skills and deliver the curriculum through the structures it may be possible to see some very real progress within six months in a primary school, years five and six, or in the fourth term of a secondary school. The struggle that this takes for teachers when they embark on this path should not be interpreted as the method failing. The students have often had years to learn habits of survival, and to learn to be dependent on the teacher for both classroom organisation and for sorting out disputes. This is called *Learned Helplessness,* (Seligman, 1975) and in our view it starts to account for the difficulty that students face when they are asked to take responsibility for themselves. If teachers can weather through these difficult times they will come to watch a class grow into a group of mature, reflective, co-operative, task oriented pupils.

When you are first introducing this work the pupils may well resist doing things your new way. This seems to be because this way of teaching and learning is more cognitively demanding than usual, as well as demanding the use of social skills. It certainly is not 'busy work' for the students, it is hard work. Two case study comments illustrate this: 'I hate it in your class miss, you have to really think in 'ere' was the response of a year 10 student. Year 5 and 6 students reported the next day that they were really tired – this was after a whole day of working in this way.

In order to help yourself through the period of 'change' it may be helpful to use observation on a regular basis. Try to get a supportive colleague to come in and gather some baseline data – number of times pupils interrupt each other, put each other down, have arguments in the class, come to you for help with little organisational matters which should really be their concern.

Alternatively you can video the group by just placing a video camera in the corner of the room with no film in for a day or two until they get used to it, then filming, or you can set them a problem solving exercise to do and video them doing it, then repeat with a different but similar exercise in a few months time. It is useful to share progress details about whole class behaviour with the group, as this constitutes real and relevant feedback which is helpful for their self-esteem. When embarking on a whole school policy approach to this way of working therefore it may be appropriate for each year team to take responsibility for different clusters of skill, in emphasis only.

If starting out alone you need to be kind to yourself and recognise that 'Rome was not built in a day' and pupils who are older will be harder work unless they have had some skills training as younger children.

If you decide to start with your own skills training first rather than teaching the skills to the students, it will inevitably mean that the behaviour of the pupils will not change, but you need to recognise that it is not their fault. The blame will have shifted away from a within-child perspective to one where you as teachers can recognise that the problem is to do with the environment, but that you cannot do much about it at the moment.

Whole school policy

In our view a whole school policy approach to managing difficult behaviour and bullying should be accompanied by quality training, which should incorporate skills training for the teacher and skills training to show teachers how to teach pupils.

We hope that the rather lengthy rationale presented in the previous chapters will go some way towards persuading managers of the importance of a long term commitment to training, and will also be helpful to those who have already started to work in this way and who are being quizzed about it by their colleagues. What we find is: nothing succeeds like success, for teachers and pupils alike!

CHAPTER 4

Making Rules

In our earlier exploration of children who have been labelled emotionally and behaviourally disturbed we have discussed the nature of their disruption in the classroom. Many of these children have difficulties at school because they fail to conform to the rules of that environment. Most children observe the behaviour of others in a school environment and assimilate the norms of behaviour into their own. As noted earlier this tends to be easier for middle class children whose background norms are similar to those of the educational establishments. Some children, however, do not.

If teachers up to now have not examined their own rule motivation and formation, if they have not examined the rule system that they use themselves, then they need to do so before they make the rules explicit to the pupils. Many of our teachers find, when they start to discuss rule formation with children, that they are simply operating a frame of rules dictated by their own experience as pupils, which are not appropriate – and perhaps never were.

The importance of rules for pupils with emotional and behavioural difficulties

Teacher skill: making rules explicit

In schools we rely heavily on the children realising what we believe they should do and, as our own action research with teachers shows, little regard is paid to explaining rules until they are broken. There are numerous examples of rules which it is easy for children to break through an inability to think as the school and teachers do. What is often highlighted in an independent inspection is the lack of consistency of rules and also the levels of sophisticated differentiation as to when a given rule is in operation or not. It may appear to an outsider as if we deliberately make it difficult for pupils to comprehend many school rules. An action that is permissible at one time is not permissible at another, for reasons that are sometimes quite obscure to pupils.

Talking out of turn (TOOT), which, as noted earlier, is the behaviour cited by teachers as the one they have to deal with most often, is a clear minefield for pupils who find it difficult to pick up the conventions and hidden rules operating. The use of rhetorical questions, eye gaze, a smile and a nod of the head to indicate that it is all right to answer, the frown that indicates that it is not permissible to answer, are very subtle rules which many children find difficult to learn. The changes in volume that children are expected to achieve in a variety of sizes of group and situations are bound to trip up many of our students. The hidden rules of when to talk, to whom and how are rarely made explicit and yet those children who continue to misunderstand them are labelled as disruptive. For example a 'no talking' sign was observed by one of us in a language classroom. The 'disruptive' label suggests that pupils 'talking out of turn' is a deliberate flouting of the rule, when in fact it might be an inability to understand it.

The results of being unable to keep a rule are damaging for pupils because their self-esteem is affected. They start off in reception class wanting to get it right. As they fail to keep these rules they receive feedback that they are 'naughty' children. This then becomes their own picture of themselves. Without specific work with these children to help them to know how to keep school rules or conventions they will keep adding to their self image of 'bad' children and as self-consistency theory shows, they will seek to maintain this self image, and in time will appear to deliberately break rules in order to maintain it. As their self-esteem falls and their self image becomes more and more entrenched, the pupils do indeed need to perform more and more outrageous rule breaking acts in order to maintain the level of feedback that they need to feel important and noticed. Even teachers become tolerant of particular levels of bad behaviour and indeed cease to notice the behaviour which is 'usual' for a particular child. This is a truly vicious circle.

Teaching the rules

In order to change the poor behaviour, many of the educational psychologists who work in schools would suggest a clear set of parameters for the child and a consistent approach to enforcing these limits. Good behaviour is then rewarded and bad behaviour either ignored – which we feel is a fairly impossible task in the classroom – or punished. We would fully endorse the need for these children to have a clear and unambiguous set of rules with consistent applications of reward. We have however found that there is a problem for these children in the way in which the rules are presented, which is often very confused and ambiguous indeed.

In the authors' experiences there have been problems where this behaviour modification approach has been introduced to the classroom. Pupils have failed to change their behaviour. It seems to us that this is because the approach makes reward depend on the child actually keeping the rules she has broken in the past: this is problematic if she has broken the rules because she doesn't really understand how to keep them.

If, for example, the pupil often runs off when she feels angry or upset then the contract will probably be to get a reward when she does not run off, but this presupposes that the pupil can develop other more appropriate ways of expressing her feelings and that the rest of the group will respond positively when she does. The chapter on 'feelings' goes into this in more detail.

Whilst the authors agree with writers like Canter and Canter (1976), that rule formation, boundary setting and explicit statements about rewards and sanctions are good practice, we go one step further in advocating that the pupils themselves should be involved in the rule formation.

We believe that for pupils with emotional and behavioural difficulties, and for the benefit of many others too there are clear steps that need to be taken:

- The hidden rules that trip up so many pupils should be openly explored in a fairly lengthy rule formation exercise.
- Next the pupils need to be given a chance to explore what 'keeping the rule behaviour' looks like when it is done.
- Finally they need to be given opportunities to try keeping the rule, whilst the teacher talks openly about the rule and what it is for.

For children who have failed to understand the rule whilst in its subtle, hidden form, this exploration might take time and will probably need a variety of approaches such as talk, art and drama to encourage understanding.

Rules of the school, the classroom and society need to be taught just as other curriculum areas are taught. Rules that are hidden, often seen as mere conventions, need to be brought out into the open.

Some conventions are better covered by whole school policies, layout of work on a page in secondary schools for example can be very confusing indeed, a whole school convention can bring in consistency and avoid time wasting confrontations about width of margin and underlining of headings.

There should be a deliberate and structured approach to demonstrating how you would behave when you were keeping the rule and what you would be doing when you did not. It is the responsibility of each teacher to ensure that their own hidden rules and conventions are opened up at the beginning of a year so that all pupils have equal opportunities to keep those rules. Telling someone your rules is not the same as teaching them what you mean by them.

Additionally we advocate the teacher making clear statements about the rules for the structures in these exercises which in their turn help the pupils to learn the skills they need to function effectively in the classroom group: in other words the skills they need to keep the social rules of the classroom. Rules for brainstorming, pair work, listening behaviour, working in groups should be made very clear to the pupils. The way in which this can be done is outlined in the exercises on Rule Formation.

The activities below demonstrate ways in which this can be achieved. These activities should ideally be undertaken at the start of a year, or when a group is just forming, and should be returned to if there is a problem with one particular rule being broken at any point in the year. They can however be undertaken with good effect at any time. They are activities which are easily transferred to any age group with the minimum of changes in format. Class teachers and subject specialists alike have followed this format and have reported positive results from all their students but particular benefits for students who have previously behaved in a difficult manner. Time given to this will not be wasted, but should be regarded as an investment. It will reduce the amount of time spent on dealing with rule breaking throughout the rest of the year.

Making a Classroom Charter
Learning to work together and negotiate in groups

The activity below addresses the making of a Classroom Charter. It also models certain structures which will later be used for curriculum delivery. The structures themselves:

- have distinct purposes
- model certain types of behaviour which are desirable;
- allow safe practice of certain skills.

Skills such as:

- face to face listening with eye contact;
- turn taking;
- taking responsibility for your own rule keeping

are important to those children who are finding keeping school rules very difficult.

The end product of this exercise is important as the classroom rules will be displayed for the whole year:

The process by which the rules are agreed is also important since:

- these are the agreed rule of the class group, not the teacher's rules; this means that the pupils have worked out for themselves the reasons for having the rules and they know that they are not there just to support the power of the teacher or on an adult's whim;
- they are not mere platitudes but are rules which the children understand in concrete terms of behaviours and situations;
- they can be referred to when broken as 'your rules' not 'my rules' when disputes and crises occur, either by the teacher or the peer group and this in itself acts as a reinforcer that the rules for behaviour are for the benefit of everyone in the group as well as for the benefit of particular individuals.

The following 'Making A Charter' activity is broken down into a series of smaller activities which can be slotted into any part of the curriculum at the beginning of a new group.

Random Two's: Initial Ideas for the Classroom Charter
Pupil skills: Learning to work with one another in pairs

Organise the pupils into random pairs. Our strong recommendation for getting pupils into random pairs is the use of cards, either a pack of playing cards or a set of 'home made' cards. If thought is given to the cards used for random two's these can be then used to make random fours later. For example, if shapes are used there can be two red triangles and two blue triangles, two red squares and two blue squares, etc. For pairs the two blue triangles can form a pair, for fours all the triangles can join together.

If teachers then mark one of each type of card with a star, using two different colour stars, they will be able to use the same cards for making alternative pairs or for indicating which child should speak first. For example, you can tell all those with red stars on to speak first, whilst those with blue stars listen; this creates the framework for turn taking exercises.

In their pairs, ask pupils to sit face to face, either on chairs or on the floor. Emphasise the posture and position for listening effectively. There are rules which you need to establish for this activity. Do not keep these as hidden rules but spell them out, very openly. Explain what the rule is, and why you want them to have this rule. Do not say 'Listen to each other'. Do say 'Sit facing each other, make sure you can look at the other person's eyes easily, lean slightly forwards so you look like you are listening, speak in turns and don't interrupt the other person, wait until they are finished.'

Figure 4.1   Random two's

Do not allow the pupils to sit side by side at a desk or table as this encourages very poor listening posture and no eye contact. Eye contact is vitally important if you wish children to hold each other's attention and ensure that they are able to stay on task. Desks and tables are easily moved to accommodate this if the teacher wishes. Once the pupils have got used to this way of working the moving of furniture can be introduced as one of your rules. Alternatively, floor spaces for whole circles take only minutes once the children know what you want them to do, so you can do this anywhere. It is worth considering booking open spaces like the hall in the initial stages of this kind of work.

Tell the children that they have three minutes to verbally brainstorm rules that they know, in or out of school. If brainstorming is new to your children explain that it's anything that you think of, even if you think its not quite right and no one can be told by the other that it is not right. Make sure that you do not give children anything with which to write at this point as you want them to listen to and look at each other (figure 4.2).

Re-form the children into the alternative pairs i.e. the red triangle with a star with the blue triangle with the star. The new pair are to verbally brainstorm the rules that operate in this classroom. Again, allow no writing and limit the time to three minutes. The 'no writing' rule is essential for the children who have behavioural problems associated with failure to read and write as they are likely to revert to old disruptive behaviour at the sign of a pen!

Teachers might like to raise the issue of hidden and open rules and give a few illustrations from their own school or classroom. Remember that whilst there are some rules in our society which are written down, a few more are unwritten and open and a great many hidden, which is why some of our children find such problems in keeping to them.

For example, hidden rules about dress codes abound: lunch time personnel in authority do not wear smocks, whilst men in suits and ties are in charge. The process of this exercise will bring the reality of this statement home to many teachers, and may help them to see just how much our institutions run on unspoken norms.

Figure 4.2   Alternative pairs brainstorm rules

Working in fours: verbal brainstorm and sorting ideas for the Charter
Pupil skills: Learning to work with one another in fours

Ask the children to join with the other pair to form a four (all four triangles). This grouping is deliberate. It means that each child has already shared ideas with two other children in the four. In this way you are creating a gradual, safe environment for 'risk taking' which is very important for children who do not relate well to their peers, especially when in a group.

In their fours, ask the children to share all the ideas they have come up with so far. Tell them that they have ten minutes.

Remind the groups of the rules for working in small groups (as outlined in the previous chapter), you may want to have these posted up on the wall for reference. In particular, emphasise the 'no put down' rule (anything that makes someone feel bad) only 'push ups' (things that encourage or compliment) are allowed.

Giving the group the responsibility for ensuring that these simple 'group rules' are kept has the effect of modelling the 'taking personal responsibility' which children with behavioural difficulties often find so hard. Modelling by peers who are also giving personal and direct positive feedback is one of the most effective ways of getting change in behaviour which lasts, as the research evidence on peer tutoring shows. Again, you are allowing the children to practice being responsible for keeping to the rules in a small, safe, environment that has a great deal of structure provided by the teacher.

Asking the pupils to share their ideas again might at first appear repetitive to the teacher, but the purpose of this structure is to allow the pupils the opportunity to rehearse the expression of a personal opinion in the comparative safety of a pair and then practice it in a four. This outcome needs to be shared with the pupils also. In our classrooms, expressing an opinion is a high level skill (National Curriculum English) but one which is sometimes actively, though not deliberately, discouraged by many teachers. Pupils are more usually engaged in the game of 'guess what is on the teacher's mind', with the teacher having all the right answers!

At the end of the ten minutes extend the task by asking each group to say what they think each rule that they have come up with is for. You may want to give them some suggestions such as safety rules, fairness rules, teacher's sanity rules!

An alternative to verbal discussion of ideas is to give each group one large sheet of paper and a pen for each member. One pen each is important for the idea of brainstorm because it allows everyone equal access and avoids scribes changing your wording and consequently your meaning.

When the time comes for adding the purpose for each rule these can be added to the sheet. The sheet can then be physically cut up and rearranged for the next part of the process. Stress the importance of everyone's ideas being represented in the final rules.

Using cards: The group consensus:

Pupil skills: Learning to negotiate with one another in fours, when the emotional content is low

At this point the group can be given cards on which to record their ideas.

Cards rather than paper are suggested for two reasons. Cards can be shared around to help the children to take turns in writing, reporting back, etc. Also cards are small and make it clear that it's the ideas that the teacher wants and not lots of writing. This is an alternative hidden curriculum message to the one normally given out in school, 'You've had a good time, now write about it'. An advantage of not asking the children to write until they are at this point is that repeated rules or unimportant aspects will have been filtered out by the sharing mechanism, whilst still allowing all children to be heard.

The group are to write on the cards in short note form (or illustrate with a drawing), the rules and who or what they are for. The cards can then be sorted by types of rules.

Each group should arrive at two to four core rules. Using the card symbols, ask group members to identify a spokesperson for each group, for example the colour of the stars might denote the spokesperson. Again, choosing in this way allows children to practice being spokesperson even if they would never have volunteered. For some children with behaviour problems or learning difficulties this might be an opportunity to be successful in a way that they have not had before, just because they are never chosen by their peer group.

Whole class circle: reporting back

Pupil skill: Learning to work with one another in a whole class group

Ask the children to sit in a circle, with the small groups adjacent to each other. Each spokesperson, with the cards as prompts, is to share what their core rules were. The teacher's job, or a child if one likes this kind of task, is to record exactly what is said. Ensure that the exact wording is used so that the teacher does not interpret the group's rule to fit their own understanding but pays attention to exactly what is said by the children.

Some teachers find the prospect of children reporting back in a group daunting. What begins in an orderly fashion ends up a 'free for all' which is very frustrating to all concerned. One structure which helps children to understand the nature of a report back is to issue small tokens (one or two of each to each child) with an '!' on some and a '?' on others. The '!' allows children to give additional information of their own and the '?' allows them to ask a question. Children have to pay for any interruptions with a token. This has the effect of silencing the more vocal members and encouraging the quieter ones. Once the students understand the purpose of such tokens and see how they fit into their own framework of fairness and unfairness they will start to design their own tokens or their equivalent.

Negative to positive rules

Pupil skill: Learning to negotiate with one another when the emotional content is low

Most of the rules will probably be in their negative form: 'You must not....'

The Negative Rules Sheet (figure 4.3) is a copy of the rules produced by some of the pupils with whom we worked and is a good example of this negativity.

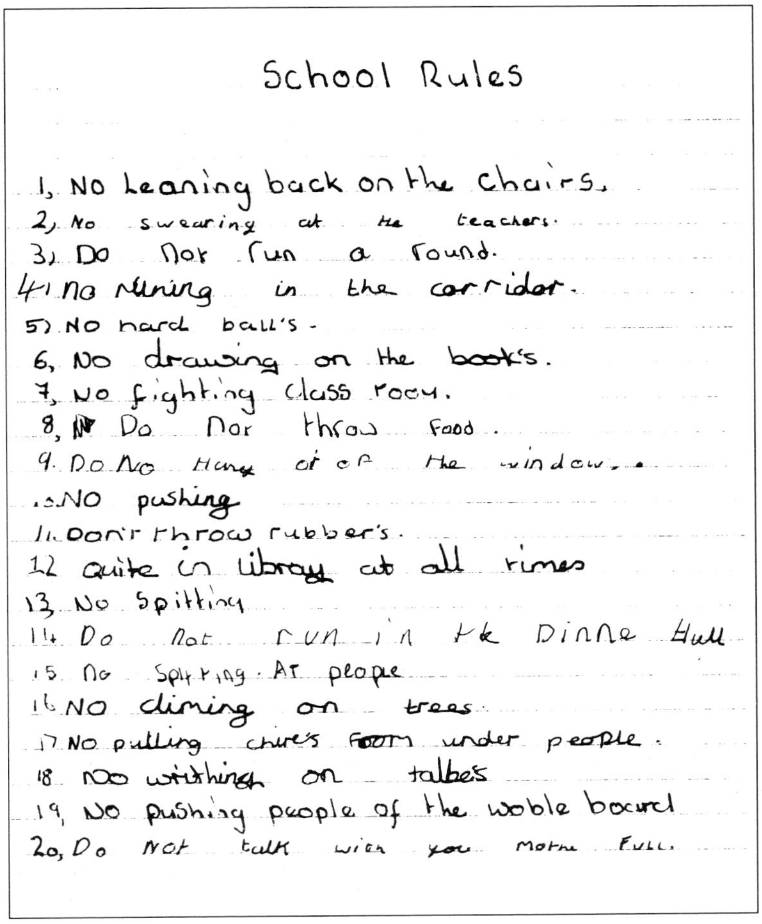

School Rules

1, No Leaning back on the chairs.
2, No swearing at the teachers.
3, Do Not run a round.
4, no running in the corridor.
5) NO hard ball's.
6, No drawing on the book's.
7, No fighting class room.
8, Do Nor throw Food.
9. Do No Hang out of the window.
10 NO pushing
11. Don't throw rubber's.
12 quite in library at all times
13, No Spitting
14. Do Not run in the Dinne Hall
15. No Spitting At people
16 NO climing on trees.
17 NO pulling chire's from under people.
18. No writhing on talbe's
19, No pushing people of the woble board
20, Do Not talk with you mothe Full.

Figure 4.3 Negative rules sheet

As a class, go through all the rules and ask the children to group them again. You might want to mark each rule with a symbol of some sort to denote the group. Ask the pupils to re-word the rules, group by group, into a positive statement. e.g. 'Don't steal' might become: 'Respect and look after the property of others'. The Positive Rules Sheet (figure 4.4) is an illustration of this; note that each rule starts with please – an interesting hidden curricula indication of what the pupils feel constitutes a positive environment.

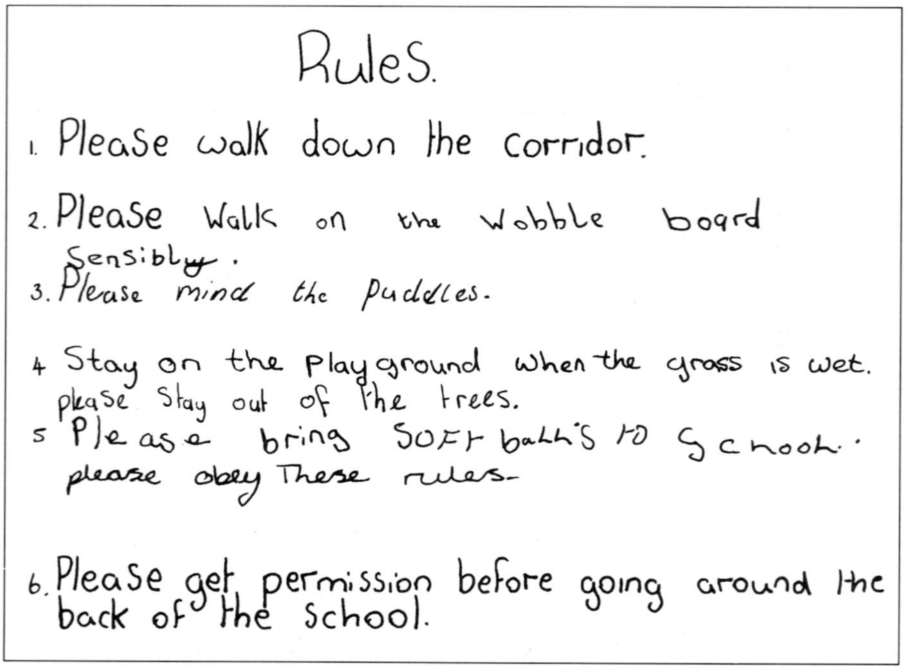
Rules.

1. Please walk down the corridor.
2. Please Walk on the wobble board sensibly.
3. Please mind the puddles.
4 Stay on the playground when the grass is wet.
please Stay out of the trees.
5 Please bring soft ball's to school.
please obey These rules.

6. Please get permission before going around the back of the school.

Figure 4.4 Positive Rules sheet

Ask the pupils to return to their original groups and write a list of 'Don't rules' which they then turn into 'Do rules'. You may wish to use the photocopiable sheet provided, figure 4.5.

Posters – displaying the rules
Pupil skills: Learning to work with one another in fours

You should arrive at between six and ten positive rules, which the children understand, in their terms. Give each group one of the rules and ask them to design a reminder poster of that rule with illustrations of situations it might refer to, which will be put in the classroom. Displaying the posters will then allow a constant reminder of the agreed rules for the whole year to be referred to when any are broken.

Our Charter

Finally each group can be asked to fill in the Charter Sheet (figures 4.6 and 4.7), which can be photocopied and adapted for many different situations using the page of different inserts.

Our Group's Ideas for Rules for the

•••••••••••••••••••••••

Don't _____

Don't _____

Don't _____

Don't _____

_____

Changing the Don't Rules to Do Rules

Do _____

Do _____

Do _____

Do _____

Do _____

Figure 4.5   Changing Don't Rules to Do Rules

Figure 4.6 Charter sheet

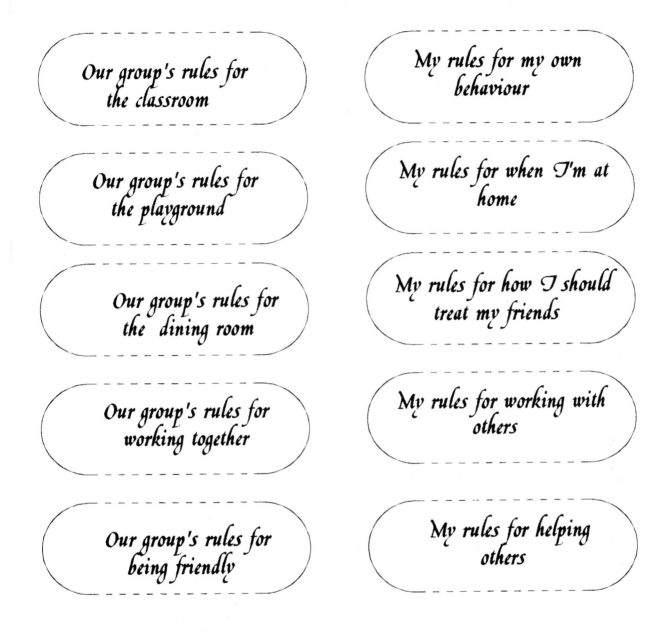

These titles can be used in conjunction with the Charter. Many others are possible. Cut out and stick these titles onto a photocopy of the blank Charter prior to photocopying for the pupils.

Figure 4.7   Titles for Charter sheet

Follow up activities on rules and punishments

Having displayed the rules, if there are big problems with children breaking them, it will because they do not yet know how to behave to keep them. With the rules displayed, teachers can work in several ways to explore more fully the aspects and implications of each of the rules. A preferred way is through role play and drama, but story telling (individual or group), story writing to illustrate a rule, letter writing to imagined people who have broken rules, drawings or cartoons to illustrate scenarios when the rules are broken are all ways to explore the issues.

Some classes might like to use the next session to consider sanctions and rewards for rule breaking and keeping. The same type of structure can be used. Classes who formulate their own sanctions and rewards are more likely to see them as fair and so ensure sanctions are easily applied by staff. All you need to ensure is that they are not overly zealous. The punishments (figure 4.8) sheet is an illustration of the work of Year 5 and 6 pupils.

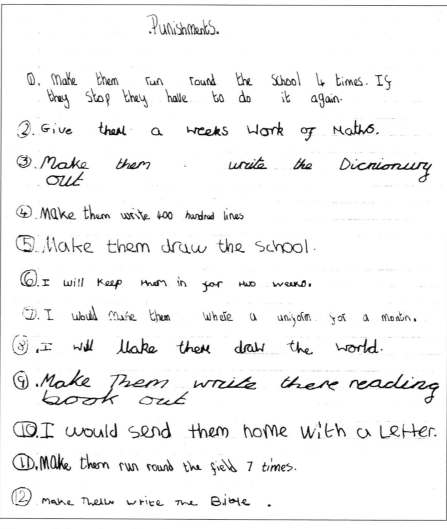

Figure 4.8   Sanctions for rule breaking

CHAPTER 5

Teaching Rules Through the English Curriculum

Curriculum applications focus on English

Having created a classroom charter and undergone the process of rule making, the pupils can explore through similar structures rules for other areas of the curriculum. It is our view that it is possible to do this for any curriculum area. For example, the rules for number in maths, particularly for patterns of number, the rules for the chemistry side of science in terms of atomic tables, formation of gases and so on. The basic structures: random pairs, brain storming – re-forming, fours, sharing, ordering, sorting and prioritising, whole circle feedback, group presentation – poster, drama, newspaper, pottery or lego model, are the same.

The curriculum area we have chosen to focus on here is English. In so doing we are addressing another hidden rule, that is, if faced with a long and difficult and, for many pupils, boring text, the curriculum delivery must be long and boring too. Some of our colleagues when faced with the new literature list, which included dense text by Hardy and Austen for their classes of relatively poor readers, reverted to the way they had been taught such texts at school – reading round the class and comprehension activities to form some kind of summary. It seems to us imperative that when faced with boring content the delivery must be imaginative and creative to compensate, this can then become an open rule that is shared with the youngsters and which they can contribute to. One author used to encourage her students to organise blockbuster and 'what's my line' games to reinforce factual information cramming for history – a strategy usually reserved for ends of terms and usually organised by the teacher. Once the students gain the skills for working in pairs and fours the possibilities for self organisation are endless.

Rationale for reward systems
Teacher skill: Praise, reward and feedback

Whilst reward tends to be quite correctly associated with positive reinforcement, in most teachers' minds, punishment is incorrectly associated with negative reinforcement.

A negative reinforcement is something which means that the student is less likely to repeat the behaviour again. If punishments worked as negative reinforcers we teachers would not have problems, nor would we be labelling children as having emotional and behavioural difficulties. The authors argue that the use of punishments with students with emotional and behavioural difficulties is counter-productive. For children who behave badly a lot of the time there is a constant stream of punishments and sanctions. There seems to be less and less good behaviour to reward. As bad behaviour increases children tend to become more and more difficult and punishments need to be more and more severe to have any effect.

Reward, then, is what we recommend that teachers focus on.

Some teachers have voiced to us their anxiety about rewards, they either feel it is unethical to give rewards at all or else they feel that to select a few students and single them out for doing something that all the others can already do is unfair.

The authors think it is useful to make the distinction between tangible rewards and praise. Tangible rewards are things like sweets, trips to special places, or privileges – such as making coffee, 'choosing time', leaving school early. Many teachers are familiar with token systems which represent steps towards these tangible rewards. Praise on the other hand is teacher approval, positive, enthusiastic feedback from the teacher which as noted earlier, if used in a specific way will help to change and enhance the pupil's self-esteem.

The authors would argue that rewards in the shape of teacher praise and encouragement are happening in the classroom all the time. In fact one of the strongest reasons for having a clear classroom reward system that is shared with students, and obvious to all, is because it is a fairer and more open system than the rewarding which is going on anyway, in an unsystematic way.

Examples of rewards that happen in an unsystematic way: teachers' smiles, teachers saying 'good,' and 'well done', teachers touching children in an appropriate way to communicate affection, such as touching the shoulder, teachers' eye contact, teachers' nods, teachers standing near to your table or seat in an encouraging way, teachers helping you.

One way to see if this list is true and to see variations in your own classroom is to ask the children; give them a questionnaire and ask them how they know when they are doing something right, or how they know if the teacher likes them or likes other children.

If this list of teacher behaviours is outside the teacher's awareness and is the only rewarding that is happening then it is bound to be unfair. If, however, teachers become aware of their own praise, and start to combine the use of it with token representations of their praise, then praise can be used in a systematic way to raise the self-esteem. In addition, because peer influence is so powerful, particularly as an influence on self-esteem, in our view everything possible needs to be done to utilise the positive voices of peers and stop the one with difficulties being removed.

Praise can be used as a way of getting the student to 'hear' positive feedback, which as outlined earlier will help shape the self-esteem. Praise which is going to change self-esteem must be

- specific;
- accurate;
- realistically tied into something the child has actually done.

Teachers might feel that some children do nothing that earns praise. It is the view of the authors that this might be more to do with the teacher's notion of what is praiseworthy than with the child's lack of good qualities.

Teachers might need to review the type of behaviour that earns teacher praise. For instance, a very untidy child might choose to underachieve because every time they write it is untidy and they receive criticism. In order to avoid those bad feelings about themselves as an untidy writer they would rather not write. They still get chastised for being lazy but in themselves they know that this was through their own choice not because there is anything bad about them. This is a fairly normal and healthy way of protecting the self-esteem; a drive that all of us share (Maslow 1970).

The teacher can make a difference to the child or student by outlining a new set of praiseworthy attributes which allows the child to succeed because the teacher has changed their praise system. John Holt recognised this in his book *How Children Fail* (1964), and introduced the Writing Derby, which was a competition to see who could write the most in a given amount of time each morning – for this particular exercise handwriting and spelling were not important.

Indeed when it comes to spelling there are much more effective methods for teaching than teacher correction on a piece of work. Co-operative group methods where pupils were responsible for coaching each other so that when their collective scores were compared there was an overall group winner proved to be well worth trying. (Johnson and Johnson 1987).

Teachers are the source of most of the feedback on academic achievement. Therefore teachers need to ensure that their praise is:

- awarded for a wide variety of required behaviours;
- helping children with emotional and behavioural difficulties by rewarding the behaviours that they can do;
- encouraging independence and personal responsibility rather than teacher dependence, as this is both de-motivating for pupils and exhausting for teachers.

To achieve this we recommend that teachers target their praise at behaviours such as:

- Helping: 'Well done Tracy for helping Wayne with his spelling'; 'Well done Tim for telling Dave the project marking criteria, I expect that has helped you to clarify them for yourself too hasn't it?'
- Calming someone down: 'Well done Michelle for helping Deanne out of her bad mood, I could see she was really fed up when she came in this morning, you've done very well there'.
- Praising the efforts of another: 'Steven you did very well in your support of Mark's story, you really looked out for the bits he had improved on, that's brilliant'.

Figure 5.1 Certificates for good behaviour

68

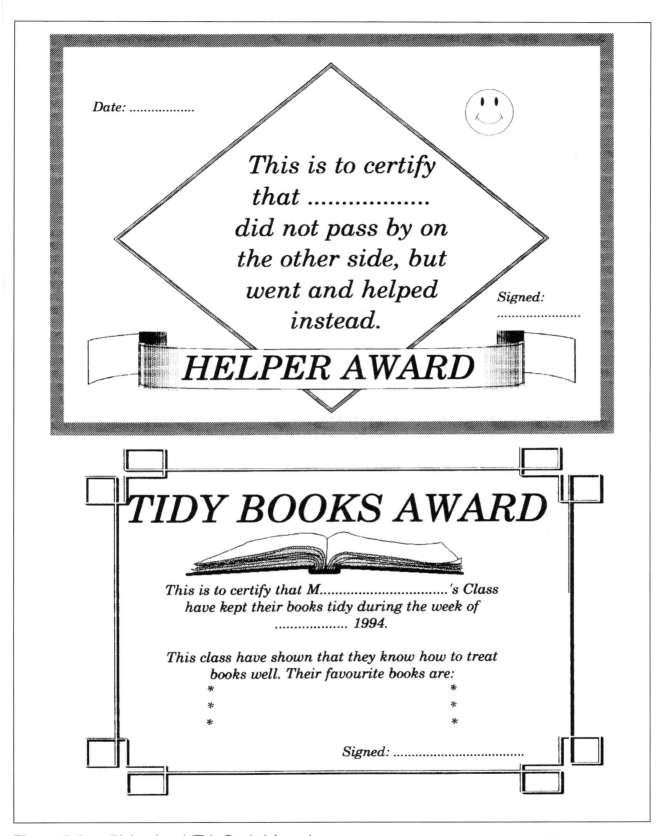

Figure 5.2 'Helper' and 'Tidy Books' Awards

Figure 5.3   'Good at being helpful' Award

- Any other behaviour which is a clear illustration of support for the class rules, for example, tidying up, putting litter in the bin, re-organising the classroom after talk and circle time activities.

To support this praise rewarding system we recommend the use of certificates, for example, the 'Certificate for Being Helpful' on the photocopiable sheet could be given for any one of the examples above. The 'Tidy Award' and the

'Litter Award' illustrated on the other photo-copiable sheets can be linked to classroom charter rules. (Figures 5.1 and 5.2). The 'Certificate for Being Helpful' (figure 5.3), can be specifically applied to 'Sorting Out Arguments' which then reinforces the kind of independence we wish to see in the students.

Public declaration of the praise

Teacher skill: Praise reward and feedback

Although writing certificates and using reward systems may seem like a lot of added work, the use of the peer group can minimise this. The effect of having praise written down is similar to being praised publicly. Too often bad behaviour is publicly reprimanded and recorded whilst good behaviour merely receives as discreet pat on the back. For children who have behavioural difficulties it is vital that the rewards are as public and as documented as the reprimands.

Many of the suggestions for rewards outlined in the exercises below can be used in conjunction with Records of Achievement Folders. Certificates awarded by staff can be included in the child's profile. Also to be included should be a record of the peer group rewards. This can be done by directly using the slips, petals etc. but might be extended into a more formalised prompt sheet for peers to give positive information about each other. Self reflection sheets for the pupils themselves to think about and record their achievement in keeping the rules should also be available. An important aspect of rewarding changing behaviour and rule keeping is to include the non-teaching staff of a school. Secretaries and lunch time supervisors often see children when teachers do not. If a simple certificate, designed to be given from other adults in school and home, is made available then all 'good behaviour' can be recorded and rewarded.

As outlined previously, many pupils with emotional and behavioural difficulties have associated reading and writing problems. The use of computers in the classroom allows I.T. across the curriculum. Pupils can be involved in designing their own certificates as part of their I.T. and English curriculum. This use of I.T. in the context of certificates can lead to children being involved in all sorts of other data gathering activities.

They can carry out surveys and interviews which are looking at marking policies and the variety of assessment criteria used in different subjects and classrooms. An investigation of the praise and rewards systems in use in the curriculum could involve a survey of the different types of rewards used throughout the school, a student questionnaire on what the students themselves consider a reward and what they would like more of, a teacher interview or questionnaire on their experiences as students of rewards, and their thoughts about rewards now. This type of work allows all students, but especially those with emotional and behavioural problems, a way of exploring rules and rewards rather than constantly being on the receiving end of the punishments.

One of the few books we have found useful for providing more ideas for rewards and certificates and personal disclosure work is that of Borba and Borba, *Self-Esteem a Classroom Affair* (1978). This is the best book we know of on the market, yet its limitations are that it is primary focused, American, and not curriculum related. We hope that teachers will feel inspired enough by this

71

chapter to adapt the ideas in Borba and Borba for their own age group, their own subject area and their own teaching style.

Rule breaking and the discussion of sensitive issues

Teacher skill: empathy and active listening

Youngsters who have behavioural and emotional problems may have suffered through adults breaking societal rules such as sexual taboos, rules to ensure their physical safety, as well as being subjected to threats both mental and physical. In therapeutic situations dolls and other objects are used to help children to talk about their responses to abuse of these rules. In school this can also be used to free children up to say what it is that is on their minds but that they may not have the vocabulary to express. We are not suggesting that teachers actually become therapists but that they enable children to say things that they actively wish to say, rather than bottle it up. Clearly it is vital that a whole class trusting environment has been built up so that the child can experience support, although our experience is that children will not say anything unless there is such an environment, or until they feel safe in a pair. The peer support that can be tapped into on these occasions is both powerful and moving.

Children can often talk through an imaginary character about things that are very personal to them. Strip cartoon drawings, and making and performing with 'paper bag' puppets are simple and effective classroom activities which allow children to 'speak' through their character.

Teachers need to be aware that this type of activity may lead to children talking about issues with which the teacher does not feel comfortable. Pupils exploring their experiences is normally what happens outside in the playground. These activities do not create the youngster's questions but merely bring them from the corners of the playground into the classroom, from the hidden curriculum into the open curriculum. These activities in the classroom do not force youngsters to disclose their innermost feelings, unless they are ready or desperately need to. For other pupils, it allows an insight into the way in which others think about rules and can encourage empathy between different children. Teachers should not be alarmed if pupils do this but should ensure that the usual networks for helping them as adults to cope with the statements made by the child are in place, and that the usual guidelines for child abuse are followed if material of this nature is disclosed.

Making rules

The structures selected to illustrate the curriculum delivery of English themselves offer support for disruptive children and keep any disruption within the control of the peer group. This support operates by giving the pupil with emotional and behavioural difficulties opportunities for further exploration and practise of the desired changes in behaviour.

The following activities take up the theme of rules by examining the rules and conventions used in literature. Firstly, making rules, secondly keeping rules and thirdly, rewarding rule keepers.

Making rules – Rules in stories: English focus, Literature
Pupil skill: working together in pairs and fours

Organise the pupils into random pairs then ask them to brainstorm rules.

For secondary aged pupils the focus can be the rules operating in Shakespeare's plays e.g. plot, character, script, as well as rules in a particular play. You may want to give examples to get them going:

– the scene is written at the top of each scene change;

– scripts are learnt and remain the same otherwise no one would be able to perform;

– characters who are evil get their just desserts.

For younger children use stories such as 'The Little Red Hen' and explore the social rules of sharing and not sharing. In addition, look at the literature rules e.g. repetition of the question. Children will be able to think of other stories that use the same techniques.

In re-formed pairs, to develop the theme, ask the children to brainstorm the social rules that the characters obey and disobey.

In fours share all the rules and group them according to whether they are social rules or rules about literature or other categories. As fours they can then add rules from other sources such as poetry, (metre and rhyme/rhythm).

They can then be asked to design posters which emphasise the consequences for breaking rules from a variety of literary sources, several Shakespeare plays or a selection of children's stories.

Teaching A classroom rule – Put Downs and Push Ups
English focus, empathetic response to Literature
Pupil skill: encouraging one another, giving and receiving positive feedback

Use the same structure of pairs, re-formed pairs, fours, to share and prioritise, and a poster or short drama to record and explore put downs and push ups in the context of literature and their real life.

Remind pupils about the 'No put down' rule and encourage them to practise 'push ups' throughout the session. In pairs, brainstorm the language of put downs and sarcasm.

In re-formed pairs brainstorm the destructive effect on characters in a story from put downs and push ups. As a four, choose one put down and one push up to illustrate. To encourage empathy, dramatise or show in a cartoon strip story how they think characters in stories are feeling (what do they say and what do they think?) when they use sarcasm.

Finally, use a large class circle to allow every member to say how they themselves feel when they use put downs and the when they are put down.

Finish with a circle where youngsters say how they feel after a push up. It is useful to get pupils to say who it was that gave them a push up and what they said. They can then record this on the photo-copiable sheet 'Put Downs and Push Ups.' (Figure 5.4).

PUT DOWNS

Draw and write about a time when you were put down or when you put someone else down.

PUSH UPS

Draw and write about a time when you gave someone a push up or when you were given a push up.

Figure 5.4   Put downs and push ups

74

Introduction to keeping rules – Use of Praise Tokens
Teacher skill: Praise

One of the problems for children with behavioural difficulties is that although they can talk about rules, their past experience is of not keeping the rules. In order to keep the classroom rules they have taken part in making they need to see examples of the rules in action and to practise keeping them. This needs to be done in an situation which is not 'real'. Pupils who have had difficulties in keeping any rules in the past will not be able to keep rules unless they have been able to try out new behaviour when it does not matter. They need to know what keeping the rule looks like. This can be achieved through other children modelling the keeping of the rule and/or through small role plays to illustrate the effect of keeping and not keeping the rules. For example, if a classroom rule is to put away your own equipment, those children who have put their equipment away can receive praise, without those who haven't receiving criticism. Praise can be verbal or take the form of more tangible items such as certificates, stars, 'tidy tokens' etc.

Other useful ways of allowing children to express their responses to rules and keeping them is through creative activities, such as those outlined below.

Exploring breaking rules through imaginary friends
Paper bag puppets – Pupil skill: Saying how you feel when rules are broken

Some rules in our lives, when broken, have devastating effects.

Organise the children into random groups of four. Remind them of the brainstorm of rules in literature, as above. Now ask the children to brainstorm rules that they have broken or that they have seen someone else break.

Following this second brainstorm, each child in the group is to talk about one rule breaking incident that they have written down and explain in detail the situation in which it happened.

As a group, they are to pick one situation that they feel illustrates rule breaking well. The group can then draw a strip cartoon, with speech bubbles, or make paper bag puppets (simple hand puppets made from paper bags), and act out what people say. The important part of the activity is to let the children try out the language that occurs when rules are broken. This is closely linked with the feelings that are aroused when rules are broken. (See following chapter). The activity can be repeated but this time the reverse situation should be acted out, that is, what happens when the rule is kept.

The effect of breaking rules – English focus, writing for an audience
Pupil skill: empathy with younger age children

For older children, the model of the moral tales, such as 'Aesop's fables', the 'Just So Stories' or the works of E. Nesbit, as well as many other children's books can be used as a starting point for writing. Begin by reading a selection of stories to the pupils or giving them the stories to read to each other. Help the pupils to look at the features of the story which relate to its moral content, its literary style, its targeted age group. In pairs or groups ask the children to write moral rule type stories aimed at a specific aged audience. They should be encouraged to use a planning sheet which helps them to decide on the rule, the style and the age group. It is useful if the age group they write for is one which is available to pilot the story – younger aged pupils on the same campus or site for example.

Having written the story, they can then go and read it to their 'audience' and then redraft it according to the response they receive. The final story can either be made into a book for that age group and presented to them or displayed with illustrations in a corridor where those children will be able to read or see it.

Using classics to explore breaking rules – empathy with literature
Pupil skill: saying how you feel when rules are broken

For secondary school students, literature that illustrates people obeying or breaking the rules can be explored through retelling the story (as in Lamb's Shakespeare Tales) or through drama. For example, Hardy's *Woodlanders* explores the results of unfaithfulness whilst his *Tess of the d'Urbervilles* explores the ever present themes of rape, murder and domestic violence. Shakespeare himself usually has an interesting concoction of betrayal and murder, (*Hamlet*, *Othello*, *Macbeth*), or an interesting set of 'what if' circumstances: *Midsummer Night's Dream*, *Tempest*, *Twelfth Night*.

Younger children can be read stories where rules are broken. Children's classics such as *Charlotte's Web* explore the hidden rules such as 'runts shouldn't be allowed to live', 'pigs should be killed for the food of man', 'spiders shouldn't write', 'animals shouldn't talk' – but 'all little girls grow up and begin to like boys'. Teachers will be familiar with innumerable stories that can also be used.

Again, drawings, retelling, strip cartoons, drama and puppetry can all be used to highlight the rules and consequences of breaking them. Constant use of the question, 'What would have happened if…?' will allow pupils to think about the possible alternatives of behaving in a different way. These questions can be written on cards and given to groups to allow them to change the stories or dramas according to the changes in behaviour.

Rewarding Rules

Rewarding rule keeping is vitally important for children who have difficulty in keeping to any rules. The reward systems should be more than just teacher praise. Although this is very powerful and important, it is also rather ad hoc because of the pressures of the classroom. The reward system should take into account and utilise peer group in the classroom as it is such an important source of feedback for positive enhancement of the self-esteem.

There are many systems enabling the peers to comment and reward those who are seen to be keeping the rules. Teachers may already be using some of them. Ones we have found to be very effective are as follows.

Sunflower petals and football fields
Pupil skill: giving and receiving positive feedback

This is a system of flower centres with each child's name displayed, in the classroom. Ready cut petal shapes are available. If child A sees B doing something 'good', for example being helpful, then they write or draw what they saw on the petal and stick it on that child's flower centre, and sign it. This way each piece of praise is specific to a piece of behaviour, is publicly displayed and is entirely down to a member of the peer group. Teachers can also add petals if they see something they wish to praise. Sunflowers are very useful because they can have many petals. Daisies are similar. For secondary aged pupils a football field with players; or pop groups can be used with peer writing on the back of the cut out pictures, they could even use their Records of Achievement folders as this is precisely the kind of evidence that is supposed to go into such folders.

Posting Box
Pupil skill: giving and receiving positive feedback

This is a similar idea to the sunflower. Slips of paper are available on which children can record 'good' things that they see. Again, particular rules can be targeted at different times. The slips are posted and then read out at the end of a day or week. Teachers can also write slips and post them. This reinforces the notion that rule keeping benefits the class members as well as the teacher.

Star Charts
Pupil skill: giving and receiving positive feedback

Usually when teachers use strategies such as star charts, the idea in their minds is to try to give out as many stars as possible to the one who has behavioural difficulties. Whilst this is a good idea as clearly these pupils do need encouragement, our experience is that the star system is even more effective if it is targeted at specific behaviours. In this case they would be rule keeping related behaviours, so, for example, a rule, 'being friendly', can be rewarded using the star as a token to publicly recognise the praise. Different coloured stars can be used for particular friendly behaviours, e.g. red for sharing, blue for listening, yellow for explaining etc.

Variations on reward systems
Teacher skill: giving positive feedback, Pupil skill: receiving positive feedback

Other systems we have seen used effectively are merit marks or house points; commercially available stickers for good work and behaviour; rubber stamps with good behaviour messages which are quite cheap and renewable; school produced certificates, easily made with desk top publishing; the 'golden book' where children are specially mentioned in assemblies for good behaviour or where year 10–12 students go to the Head teacher's office to sign as a result of outstanding behaviour; bronze, silver and gold awards for targeted behaviours; trips out of school for keeping behavioural contracts; responsibility given when changes in behaviour are demonstrated; free or choosing time; and letters or home school books to parents reporting on the good behaviour, instead of just letters or notes to tell of the bad.

If you still have any doubts about the value of praise and public declarations, try it and then ask the students what they think.

CHAPTER 6

Pupils with Emotional and Behavioural Difficulties and the Expression of Feelings

In this chapter we explore the nature and role of feelings, in relation to the school environment and the child with emotional and behavioural difficulties. The first issue is that of feelings themselves. Feelings are the emotions that we experience. These emotional responses are the results of our interactions with the world and the people with whom we relate. Feelings occur as a result of positive or negative experiences. They do not stand alone. If we are feeling happy or sad or angry it will be a response to a person or event. Behaviour is the way in which we try to express our feelings, this expression itself is an attempt to communicate, but this may not be in a person's awareness.

Difficulty in identifying feelings

Teacher skill: stating feelings

As mentioned in chapter one, the primary feeling is usually one of pain; our defence mechanisms mean that we experience the pain briefly then cover over the hurt with anger.

Sometimes the source of the pain is so buried underneath our own defensive mechanisms it is very hard to find. If we are asked how we are feeling, we will truthfully respond that we are angry or fed up or unhappy. Very angry pupils will probably be those who are hurting very badly. This can be very helpful as a reminder to teachers dealing with an aggressive pupil on a very bad day. The more aggressive they are, the more hurt they are likely to be feeling.

For instance, I might overhear a colleague talking about me in a detrimental way. My initial feeling is to be hurt. This is immediately followed by a feeling of anger, wanting to revenge the slight, or a feeling of worthlessness and depression, feeling unappreciated by all those around me. I might then react to those secondary feelings in a variety of ways. I might use verbal aggression to attack that colleague, I might start spreading rumours about that person to other colleagues, I might fume silently and convince myself that they are right or I might begin to behave as they have said I do.

All of these reactions fit into Dreikurs' list of goals (1968) which he says may drive us when we are feeling hurt and worthless: attention getting, power, revenge or a display of inadequacy. My feelings and my reactions are very complex and it would be very difficult for an outsider to know what behaviour was the result of which feeling. It would also be no easy task for the person herself. It would be rare for me to weigh up the accuracy of what they have said, decide what parts are and which parts are not true, and positively act to change my behaviour for the better. This is, however, what we do expect pupils to do when we reprimand them for bad behaviour! In this scenario I am unlikely to be aware of my own real motivation, that I was hurt, because it is overlaid with lots of other conflicting and easier to deal with emotions. It also explains why pupils are actually unable to answer the question, 'Why did you do that?' or even 'Why are you angry?'. In fact it is so likely that the pupil will not actually know why, that it is better if the teacher asks a different kind of question, 'How are you feeling?' or even 'Where are you feeling it?' are useful 'defusing' questions, that may help the pupil to locate their feelings.

It becomes apparent then that stating feelings is difficult for both teachers and pupils because it assumes that both parties can identify their feelings. If something is difficult we need to practice, and the practice that both teachers and pupils need is in stating their own feelings when emotions are not running high. This will mean that they will be able to call on this skill when the need for the three part message demands a statement of feeling for 'crisis behaviour' management.

Expression of feelings – behaviours

Teacher skill: identifying acceptable behaviours

Some kinds of expression of a feeling, or behaviours, are more acceptable in schools than others. Many of the pupils who experience difficulties in school have problems in relationships or with the school environment itself. School and the people in it give rise to an emotional response that is uncomfortable. Many pupils carry this feeling with them into adulthood, and still feel uneasy in schools when they are parents. The behaviour they use to express this discomfort is often the behaviour which school finds undesirable and ends up with the child being labelled 'emotionally and behaviourally disturbed'. Typical responses are physical and verbal aggression or sometimes total non-co-operation, a switching off.

In the earlier chapters we outlined the ways in which teachers often jump to conclusions about pupil behaviour and attribute motives such as attention seeking and manipulation to them.

The authors feel that not only should teachers train themselves to use behavioural descriptors rather than judgements, as outlined in chapters two and seven, they should also make it very clear to pupils which behaviours are acceptable for expressing anger. This in itself presupposes that teachers have clarified for themselves the fact that it is alright for pupils to feel anger, that it is also alright for them to express anger, and healthier to let it out than bottle it up. What is not acceptable is destruction, of self or others, or property. This may lead to an interesting discussion with the students about the role of stamping of feet, of shouting 'I feel angry', of a room with a punch-ball, of exactly what does constitute legitimate expression of feeling. This discussion could then lead on to the importance of checking out facts with each other and practical drama work along these lines could be introduced.

Feelings and the curriculum

Schools and the curriculum give very mixed messages about feelings and their place in education. A group of pupils, with one powerful adult, in a relatively small room, is a situation which is bound to elicit emotional responses.

The curriculum, whichever way it is delivered, is designed to provoke interest, excitement, thoughtfulness, sadness, happiness, and often does provoke frustration and anger. However, the teaching style that teachers choose to use rarely gives the time or the space for dealing with the range of emotional responses that this style has created. Some further conflicts in the way school indicates children should deal with emotions are sometimes modelled by the staff in school. Often you will observe a teacher displaying powerful, angry responses to classroom situations, rarely will you observe a teacher publicly showing sadness or fear. Having modelled one type of emotional behaviour, teachers must expect that some of their children will believe that behaving like that is acceptable. A teacher who models feelings, who shares his feelings by telling the pupils how he feels, is demonstrating that all of us share the experience of all the emotions. Such modelling is particularly helpful to those children who are having difficulties in coming to terms with their emotional and behavioural responses in school.

Fontana, 1992, talks about the power of modelling in his chapter on personality, whilst Hargreaves, 1967, identifies the importance of teachers saying and modelling the same thing, otherwise it is the model in the hidden curriculum that is adopted by the students and not the words of the teacher.

Teachers need to:

- constantly reinforce the 'no put down, only put ups' rule, through using both teacher disapproval for put downs and teacher praise, both verbal and token, for put ups; the compliments exercises in this chapter help to give pupils practice in giving positive feedback;

- continue to use praise in all its forms as outlined in chapter five because this represents positive feelings being expressed and is a good model to the students of positive expression of feeling;

- use the three part message to express negative feelings so that it is the behaviour that is being disapproved of and not the pupil;

- practice using 'self disclosure' when appropriate – sharing with the pupils times when they as teachers have felt similar feelings, especially embarrassment or loneliness, which are often the feelings that pupils think no adults have ever experienced.

Creating the environment for expressing feelings

As mentioned in chapter two and chapter five, the ethos is the responsibility of the teacher; they can use their own rule frames and teacher praise to make it clear that they want pupils to express their feelings.

This is an important aspect of pupils' skills training, especially for pupils who have difficulty with their emotions. Pupils need to know that the classroom is a safe place to say how you feel. Many have experienced the opposite to be true. In the past they have been laughed at or bullied for crying, and perhaps shouted at for 'being cheeky' or saying what is on their mind. They have learnt not to cry and not to say what is bothering them. The teacher needs to structure the classroom environment to demonstrate that it is safe to express personal thoughts and feelings.

The structures of pairs and fours go some way towards this. The exercises outlined below build on these prerequisite skills, so that the cycle of 'no risk taken, no trust formed' is broken through carefully graded steps. This enables the least damaged pupils to begin to take risks and state the feelings they have, thus creating trust and modelling the target behaviour for the more vulnerable. As mentioned in the previous chapter, if material of a sensitive nature does emerge it will be because the pupil wants to say something. This work does not force the pupils to say things they do not want to say, nor does it create the feelings, it merely facilitates the pupils to express their feelings.

Drama to explore feelings, reactions and their effects

Role play is a term which many teachers and some children find very threatening. They claim they do not know how to do it or what to say. The authors have found the word 'pretending' fits primary aged children more easily whilst the use of the drama studio can have powerful effects for secondary aged students, especially in lessons where they least expect it, like maths and science. Relaxation and 'imagining what would happen' prior to role play can help youngsters who find it difficult to dramatise events.

Other pupils, especially those with emotional and behavioural difficulties, have benefited from being the director of the drama but not in the drama. It is their role to explain to their group of 'actors' what they are to say and how they are to say it, how they are to move and react, what their facial expression would be and what changes there are in their body posture. This has the effect of allowing the pupil to gain an insight into their own feelings and the feelings of the other participants in events, whilst gaining status from being in a position of authority and leadership.

Role plays can arise from:

- an actual incident;
- scenarios developed by the teacher;
- from the children's own experiences or
- through peers writing scenarios for other groups to act out.

We would suggest that many pupils need to experience a number of different dramatisations of emotions before they are able to take on board the implications for themselves, so a wide variety of role play situations should be used, with many different settings and organisations. What is important for all the role play work is that the pupils use the language of feelings, since the aim of the drama is to help pupils to identify what you look like, what your expression and body posture might be, what you are likely to say, when you are experiencing a certain emotion.

The issue of interpreting other people's feelings and motives has been raised several times in the context of teacher behaviour. For pupils with emotional and behavioural difficulties it is likely that there is a mismatch between how they think they appear and how they do appear to others when they are excited, angry, or upset. Both scripted and improvised drama is a good way of allowing pupils to have a shrewd understanding of how their own body language is interpreted by others. It also helps them to learn the skill of checking out so that the number of disputes based on misinterpretation of accidents is reduced.

Paying of compliments for an accurate self-image

This is vital for pupils with behavioural difficulties. As seen in chapter one, pupils with emotional and behavioural difficulties are likely to have a low self esteem and a distorted or inaccurate self image and unusually inflated ideal self. These pupils have a negative view of themselves, even those who appear boastful. They are very quick to accept as true any negative information about themselves as this is congruent with their own, present self image. (Burns, 1982; Coopersmith, 1967; Hamacheck, 1987). They do however find it difficult to assimilate any positive information because the self image tends to be self preserving, that is, we can only accept information that is a close fit with what we already believe about ourselves. Receiving compliments from the peer group as well as praise from the teacher is important if children are to enhance their self image. As all teachers know, children (or adults) are unlikely to pay each other compliments unless the classroom is structured so that they will do so. As the way we see ourselves is based upon feedback received from a wide variety of people throughout our lives, changing or enhancing the self image will require repeated compliments and positive feedback from as many people as possible.

Counselling skills to detect the pupils' motivation

Teacher skill: active listening

We would suggest that because of the complexity of feelings surrounding anger the only way to unpack a persons' real motivation is not to assume that you already know what it is but rather to help that person to explore, layer by layer, the feelings that they have. For teachers to do this they need to be able to recognise their own feelings and separate them from their reactions. If they do not do this then they might mislead both themselves as observers, and the pupil concerned. Teachers also need to use the skills of empathetic listening, as outlined by Gordan (1974), so that they model this for the others in the class. One of the most powerful aspects of counselling skills is that of checking out the other's feelings.

Special case – boys

Teacher skill: specific skills training with boys

We have noted in earlier chapters the problems that boys have in expressing their hurt or vulnerable feelings in any other way apart from aggression. We have also noted that we feel that this may explain the disproportionate numbers of boys in special EBD schools. We might say that boys are emotionally crippled as a result of their socialisation, being unable to show their emotions or even to recognise what they are feeling. This creates very real problems for them. Many find it difficult to relate to women (a clear problem for both female parents and female teachers); some find it hard to parent in later life without aggression; some find they are getting into trouble with the law because of their level of violence; and often in school they are separated from other children by withdrawal and exclusion. It is our view that the boys probably need extra work on the skills training outlined in this book, and especially those skills of expression of feeling outlined in this chapter, over and above that carried out with the girls. It may be that particularly with older students separate gender classes are necessary to enable their particular problems to be addressed.

Rationale for exercises in the expression of feeling

The encouragement of the expression of feelings through appropriate behaviour together with the ability to do this as it arises in the school environment can be addressed through the structures below. These are based upon a developmental view of learning; which says that it is better to recognise and express one's feelings, not just react to them. This developmental approach takes children through simple self disclosure of factual then personal information. This builds up knowledge and trust within the class group, enabling further risk taking. (Rogers, 1969). Relaxation techniques, creative expression through drawing and drama then can be used to help children to identify the feelings that they have and give them useful labels. (Hall *et al*, 1990). This helps with the higher skill of expression of feelings. Structures which encourage pupils to express their feelings and practice them in real and imagined contexts are also outlined. This practice in a low threat situation is essential if pupils are to use the skill when the stakes are higher.

The programme outlined below takes children through these steps. Difficult students will have been identified because they need more time and practice at each and every stage. They will also need to frequently revisit skills. Teachers should not get frustrated when students do not transfer skills they appear to be gaining as they have a lifetime of bad habits to forget.

The work of the teacher therefore is to:

– help all the students in the class to be able to express their feelings;

– do so on a regular basis so that they practice and so that the feelings do not get stacked up ready for a violent boiling over;

– teach their students how to express their feelings in appropriate ways and then practice doing this in safe environments;

– to recognise for themselves that the feeling itself is not wrong it is just certain ways of expressing it that are not acceptable.

Practising saying feelings

All about me – Stem statements
Pupil skill: expression of feeling

This can be used with any age group. One author often used maths related stem statements for a Year 9 end of Friday afternoon maths lesson; I would feel more confident about maths homework if…I'd get on better in maths if…The bit I like best in our maths topic is…

Firstly in face to face pairs, then in fours and finally in a circle (see previous chapter) children use stem statements written on cards; the sorts of stems you need to give them are listed such as:

In school I like it when.....
My favourite meal.....
The place I most enjoyed visiting.....
The lesson that I don't like.....

My favourite thing
Pupil skill: expression of feeling

The students are asked to bring a personal item from home and then talk about it. Again, the use of two different pairs, then fours and finally a circle allows pupils to try out and then rehearse and refine what they are going to say before they have a whole class audience. For many young people this is important as they find talking in a large group stressful. This is often the case with very verbose youngsters, who talk a lot and say very little.

A 'Me bag'
Pupil skill: expression of feeling

Even quite old students (including teachers on our courses) enjoy being asked to put together a 'Me Bag', that is, a collection of items that they feel represent something about themselves. Each youngster then has an extended time to talk the group through their items, with questions asked using a '?' card system as in the previous chapter.

There will be some pupils who are initially unable to think of what they want to say. Establish, then remind pupils of the rule for circle time as outlined in chapter three, which is that they are allowed thinking time, rather than just 'pass'.

The feeling dice
Pupil skill: expression of feeling

This is another exercise that spans the entire age range. It is a simple device that

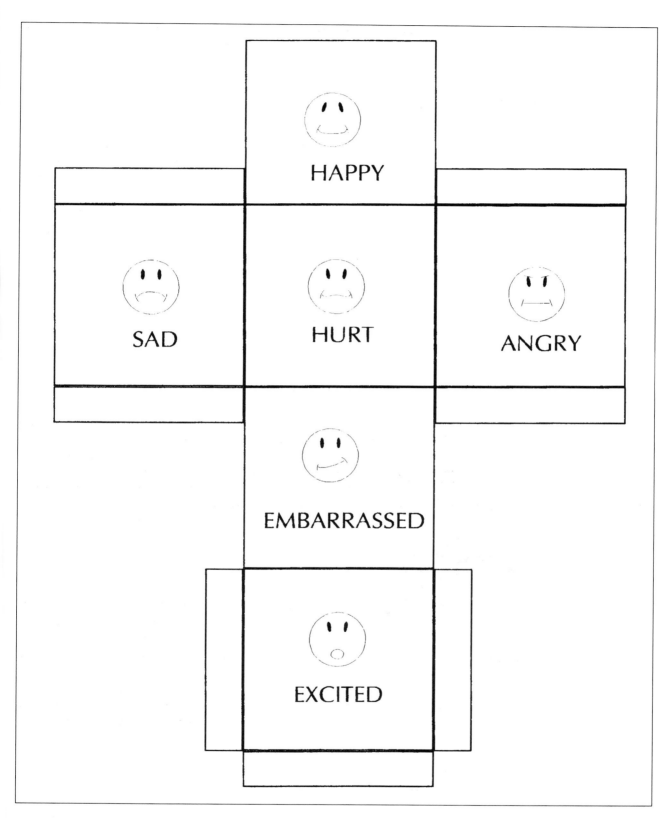

Figure 6.1   Net for a 'Feeling Dice'

facilitates the sharing of feeling statements. A net for a feeling dice is provided, figure 6.1. The students can be asked to go through a long exercise where they brainstorm feelings in pairs, prioritise and select six feelings in a group of six (three pairs join together), draw and assemble their own dice, then play it in groups of six. Alternatively they can bring their dice to the whole circle and play.

To play: the pupils take it in turns to roll the dice and complete the sentence, 'A time I felt sad/ happy/ excited this week was when...' the feeling word they use depends on the word rolled on the dice.

Our experience is that pupils ask to do this exercise over and again, confirming our belief that they are hungry for opportunities to share how they feel.

Feeling Dice game – designed by children in Years five and six
Pupil skill: expression of feeling

The children designed a board game based on the usual rules of board games, moving a token around the board, but the decision as to whether you can move on depends on you successfully completing the stem sentence from the rolling of the feeling dice. The positions moved to on the board were also feelings. So if for example you roll sad and you say 'I felt sad this week because my dog was poorly', you then move your token to the sad square.

Stem statements – advanced work
Pupil skill: expression of feeling

As the pupils gain more trust and confidence in talking about themselves it will be possible to introduce new stem statements that refer to feelings. At first it is best to mix these with previously used statements to reduce any feelings of anxiety.
Statements such as:

A time when I felt cross was.....
The most exciting day of my life was.....
Something that makes me very angry is.....
A time when I have lost my temper.....

Some kind of circle work where students say how they feel in the whole group needs to be incorporated into lessons on a daily basis in primary schools and may be every other lesson for each subject specialist in secondary school. It does not take long and can be used as a review of learning, a planning or a concept formation strategy.

In the primary phase the 'Sharing Circle' rapidly becomes the most often requested activity across the age range. Be prepared at first to spend a long time on the circle. This type of self disclosure work begins by being very time consuming, but becomes a five minute activity as the aggression in the class diminishes.

Using the activities outlined above allows pupils to gain a clearer perspective of themselves. Other activities to encourage self disclosure involve the pupils' peers giving them information about how they see the pupil.

Practising identifying feelings

Drawing and visualisation
Pupil skill: identifying feelings

Relaxation techniques are used in a wide variety of situations and are a valuable tool for the teacher. They can be taught as part of a P.S.E. programme or as part of the P.E. curriculum. Pupils can be asked to lie on P.E. mats and then quietly and gently be talked through the relaxation, or they can be asked to sit comfortably in their chairs and close their eyes. One way to start is to do a whole body tensing and relaxation exercise. Begin at the toes and ask pupils to perform a series of muscle tightening and relaxing movements working up the body finishing with facial muscles. Relaxation can be combined with guided fantasy journeys, either to a 'relaxing' place or to explore a past or imagined situation which has caused stress or discomfort. Scripts for guided fantasies are available in Hall *et al* (1990).

Visualisation of yourself doing or saying something in a situation is a good way of trying out safely a different way of behaving or responding. This relaxation and visualisation can be followed by drawing or physically acting out the situation.

An important step is to ask pupils to relax and imagine a time when they felt a particular emotion, talking them through the situation, the type of reactions they experienced, the way they looked and felt, and then immediately after they have imagined this ask them to draw what they felt. The pupils can then work in pairs to describe their drawings to each other. The effect of drawing is to capture, using the 'emotional' creative side of the brain, an image which can further help children share, recognise and explore the nature of their own feelings.

The classic response of a fourteen year old boy to the question, 'Well how do you feel about that?' is, 'I dunno.' He is probably right, he does not know how he feels. Unless students of this age explore the vocabulary for feelings and practice using a range of words to communicate a range of feelings the adolescent communication with teachers and parents will founder. It is no wonder that Records of Achievement become merely an exercise to do at the end of a module with mediocre responses written in. ROA demands an affective response from students.

There are opportunities for science and maths teachers to build affective domain and creative work into their delivery of the curriculum. It is the teacher skill and the teacher belief that this is a worthwhile activity that is the problem. Students can be asked to draw their feelings of anxiety when handling toxic acids, of excitement when an experiment works out. They can be asked to draw how they feel about the subject and its subsidiary components, which can then help to clarify for them what exactly it is about science that they enjoy and therefore what career choice they ought to make. Given the low morale amongst the medical profession – evidenced by the research showing high suicide rates, high stress-related alcohol consumption and high self reported stress levels – at the moment this is probably an important issue.

Clay model
Pupil skill: identifying feelings

A similar approach to the one above can be used with clay or other play material which is malleable, with lego or with other construction material. The pupils are asked to think of a time when they felt; angry, sad, happy or jealous, then model the feelings in the clay or build something with the lego, then share their thoughts about what they have done with a partner.

Role play re-run of an incident
Pupil skill: practising acceptable ways of stating feelings when cross

Although at first sight this exercise might look like the right material for English or primary settings, it can and should be considered for both the secondary setting and for subjects in which its usefulness is not immediately obvious. If an incident has broken out in Design, for example, the teacher can choose to use this exercise as an example of observation, reflection and re-shaping, which are in fact the processes required for the design problem, and also the skills required for working in teams and groups.

It is vital that all teachers in all subject areas take on responsibility for teaching these skills as students need them in these subject areas. Time spent on these skills will be reaped later as they start to solve their own disputes and work more constructively in the time given.

The teacher can initially provide scenarios of incidents for this activity, pupils can later start to produce their own, (see the sheets, figures 6.2–3, where the pupils have written about the incident and drawn it). These will need to be done in some detail for the children to act out. They should be based upon incidents where one person says something which their partner needs to interpret to find out what that person is really saying.

The students should work in fours, with two taking the acting role and two observing. An example scenario is given below.

A group of pupils playing in the playground with a football. The football suddenly deflates. Pupil A, whose ball it is, begins shouting 'You're dead, you are!' to pupil B, who is part of the group and whom the pupil A thinks has punctured the ball. B responds angrily, believing himself to be threatened though with no idea what he is supposed to have done. Act this scene and act out what happens next.

At the end of the drama the two observers should interview the actors. In order to help the interviewers, questions can be added to the reverse of the card, such as:

What does he really mean when he says you're dead?
What other phrases might he use ? (I'm really fed up with you.)

What does A think has happened ? (Ask actor A to say what he thinks, in his role.)

What is A feeling?

What does B think has happened ? (Ask actor B to say what he thinks in his role).

FootBALL.

There were two boys playing football and one person kicked the football and it hit another person. The other boy kicked the football and it hit some body else. Then we made friends and one boy helped the other boy up. It happed again but the second time it all came in to a fight.

WHAT SHOULD You DO?

The two boys and the bag.

One day two boys had the same bag and when it came to dinner time one boy was acting stupid and threw the other boy's bag down the stairs thinking it was his now this broke up into a fight.

WHAT SHOULD YOU DO?

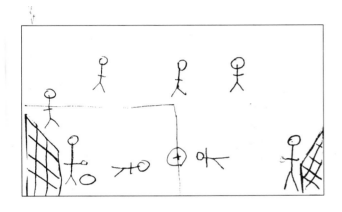

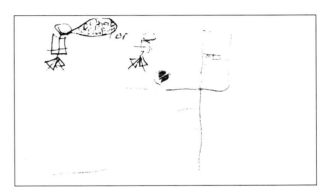

HOCKEY

All was playing hockey. One boy lifted his hockey stick up and this boy hit another boy in the face and started a fight.

WHAT SHOULD YOU DO?

THE BUMP.

3 boys were playing football and I Bumped in to one of them. He pushed me then it went in to a fight and I hit them and they hit me. So they fell on to the floor and I ran away. one of the boys ran, away after me and caught me and he got me on the floor.

WHAT SHOULD you DO?

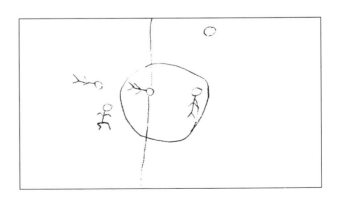

Figure 6.2   Incident scenarios

Pushing

A class are going down to assembly and all the children are pushing. one falls over and bangs their head. He thinks it someone did it on purpose and so he picks a fight with the boy he blames.

WHAT SHOULD YOU DO?

ABOUT the nEw girl.

One day me and my friend were doing our maths but we couldn't do them, so we went over to our new girl to cheat but the dinner bell went. After dinner, me and my friend got her into the toilets and the teacher came. when we got to the class room me and my friend and the new girl had a fight with paper and we made friends.

WHAT SHOULD YOU DO?

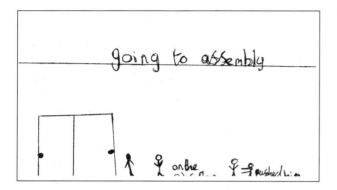

going to assembly

NAME CALLING.

There were 2 girls and 1 of the girls came over to some other kids and said that girl over there has been calling you names. We went over there to the girl and said have you been calling us names?

WHAT Should you Do?

TELLING TALES

one day there were two girls fighting. One was pulling faces at the other. The other girl said why are you pulling faces at me, she said you told somone that I took some sweets from the Shops. I was walking by so I said "what is going on"? One of the girls Said "she told someone that I took sweets from the shop."

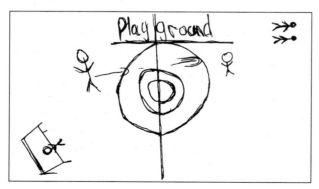

Play ground

Figure 6.3 More incident scenarios

What is B feeling?

What is the outcome?

The observers' job is then to rerun the drama up to the end of the scene and give directions to the actors to change what they say and do to reflect what they have found out about the real feelings of the players. At the end of the new drama, the observers can re-ask the questions and look for changes in feelings as well as outcomes.

Scenario cards can then be exchanged with another group and the observers can become the actors.

Expression of difficult feelings in role
Pupil skill: expressing the feelings that are hard for them

It is sometimes much easier initially to try out the expression of very difficult feelings when in role. It is a case of 'my friend has a problem…' Drama allows children with emotional difficulties to try out the vocabulary of feeling whilst still remaining apart emotionally. In a way, both they and their audience know the reality is that they do own the feeling but the role reduces the threat to their self image and esteem.

Use relaxation and guided fantasy to help the children focus on a difficult feeling, such as anger, followed by drawing the situation. Ask the director, that is the child whose drawing it is, to physically position the character, arrange their body posture and facial expression and tell them what to say, throughout the whole scene. At the end of the scene, the actors can say how each of their roles made them feel and suggest changes in the script. The director then re-runs the action with the actors contributing to the changes when necessary. When the scene has been changed to use different language the director takes on one of the roles. It doesn't really matter whether it is the role that he/she originally had in real life or another. Either way he/she will experience the difference changing what is said (changing scripts) can make to the feelings experienced.

Practising giving compliments

Dip in the bag compliments
Pupil skill: giving and receiving positive feedback for an accurate self image

The sentences for this activity are best generated by the youngsters themselves. It can be used in any curriculum area and may well rejuvenate records of achievement processes in secondary schools, especially in the year ten to eleven age range. The criteria can be carefully matched to end of module tests; so that in science, for example, the cards may have aspects of the skills that are needed for burning peanuts to measure calorific value which will be cognitive skills as well as the affective skills of helping and encouraging. This activity ends up being popular with all age ranges, once strategies for dealing with reading such as symbols or drawings have been dealt with.

On cards write or have the children write compliments such as:

This person is good at football

This person is a good friend

This person is good at calculus

This person helps me out

Use as many different compliments as you can and ensure they cover physical attributes and skills, social skills as well as academic success. Everyone is good at something. The cards are put in a bag and taken out one by one as they are passed around the circle and the compliments given. At first youngsters may only feel able to say the person's name and the compliment. Insist that the person receiving the compliment says 'Thank you' not the usual 'No I'm not'.

As they feel more able to use the compliments ask the children when giving a compliment to say at what particular incident or time that person earned the compliment. For example:

'John, you are a good friend because yesterday you shared your crisps with me when I had spilt mine' or

Rachel you were good at measuring the liquid into the test tube for titration, you didn't spill a drop whereas mine went all over the place, remember?

This progression to link compliments with behaviour is crucial because it allows children to experience making the link between what they do and how people see them. For those with difficult behaviour there is often a denial that what they actually do is what makes the difference to those around them. Whilst they lack personal responsibility for their actions and their consequences there is little chance of changing their poor behaviour. By using this activity the links of personal responsibility for behaviour and its consequences are made without the link being directly to do with them, their bad behaviour and high risk, highly emotional incidents.

Compliments consequences – Activities
Pupil skill: giving and receiving positive feedback

For pupils of all ages who are able to write this is very successful. Each student has a piece of paper which has a child's name on it and it is passed around the circle, folded down each time, and compliments written on it by the rest of the group. Each student then receives a sheet of anonymous compliments.

Compliments cocktail parties
Pupil skill: giving and receiving positive feedback

This can be done in several ways. One is to use sticky tape to attach a piece of paper to everyone's back and then pupils can circulate and write a compliment on as many backs as they can or the activity can be entirely verbal and youngsters greet each other, pay a compliment and then say thank you before they move on. If students need more structure they can use a 'carousel formation' where the inner circle remain seated and the outer circle pay a compliment and then move on one space and pay a compliment to the next person. In our experience students with a low self-esteem need to take part in compliments activities regularly in order to have a more accurate self image and increase their ability to attribute success as well as failure to themselves.

Feelings and History

Drama and history have clear potential. One of the easiest ways to allow children to experience what it would have been like in another age is to allow them to act it out. Just as role play scenario cards, (with or without questions) and relaxation, guided fantasy and drawings can be used to help pupils recognise and express their own feelings, the same structures and skills can be brought to bear on the curriculum area of History. Tudors and Stuarts, with their battles and executions, loss and grieving, the excitement and anticipation of seafarers and explorers; Victorian children's experiences of the pampered life of the rich and the working toil of the poor: whichever era pupils are studying the experience of human emotions remains universal.

Role play for portraying historical events is, however, different to role play to explore the present day personal emotions of children. Role play for History needs to be taught in a structured way. This will ensure that it is successful in promoting an understanding of the content as well as an appreciation of what life was like for people of that time. Unless Drama is used to deal with the historical factual content as well as the historical appreciation then it is likely to be time consuming rather that cost effective in terms of curriculum delivery.

We suggest that the following development of skills enables maximum learning of content with the minimum de-motivation (work sheets, writing and reading) for the difficult children whilst maximising creativity and interaction, both of which are excellent motivators.

1. Character cards for 'Rainbow Group' discussions.

Divide the class into groups of six. Give each group a set of six prompt statements or character profiles for the time to be studied, written onto cards. These should be randomly distributed in the group. Victorian characters might be a doctor, a lady's maid, a chimney sweep, a politician or teacher, a charity worker, a merchant sailor. For older children the characters might be historical figures from a period such as Queen Elizabeth I, Drake, Raleigh, Lady Jane Grey, Mary Queen of Scots etc. The six different characters then each form a character group for purposes of research. Older students might merely have the name of a character, which the group can then spend some time independently researching in detail. Younger children might be given information by the teacher which they can read about together as a group.

Having found out information about who they are and what they might have been doing, with the support of their character groups, children should re-form into their original circle to put over different points of view on a subject pertinent to the historical time. For example, these Victorian characters should first introduce themselves with information about their role and then they might like to discuss in their roles the sewers and water supply through the wells, health and disease, children's lives etc. Questions can be encouraged so that children who have not readily spoken about their character are encouraged by the group to do so.

This method of working is very cost effective in time as each 'character' has spent time finding out about one aspect of Victorian life but receives information on five others in return…and no writing. It is extremely effective with younger children. As children begin to get used to working this way all the teachers who have tried this and reported back have said how very easy it is for children to learn and how relaxing it is for teachers to teach. They have also reported that they even get time to talk to children.

2. Personal then Historical – Conflict.

The second step in historical role play is to role play a personal issue first, which is then transferred and equated with a historical situation. Teachers can choose their starting point with information sheets, television programmes, scripted drama, literature, improvised role play, fantasy and drawing.

Suggested topics for this role play might include arguing with parents, marrying or going out with a black/white partner, falling out with a friend, moving classes/school without a friend. These again can be given to groups using scenarios written on cards.

Having explored the feelings of present day situations these can then be related to Tudors and Stuarts, Catholic and Protestant, Roundheads and Cavaliers, Jews, Arabs and/or Gentiles, Europe in World War II and the holocaust, or in fact any period in history as all have their groups in conflict.

Groups who have acted out a modern day conflict re-enact the same conflict but as if it took place during the period that is being studied. If children have not yet acquired any information about the period, study groups, such as in the previous activity can be used, either with information provided by the teacher or resource books available.

3. Role Play to Encourage Empathy – World War I.

The culmination of historical drama is to create an empathy for the time being studied. It is suggested that groups are formed in a similar way to the rainbow groups above. However, this time they research their 'character group' and script a short drama/documentary describing their lives, their views, their prejudices, their feelings, from entirely their character's perspective. Groups could represent the German Officers, the English Officers, the wives back home, the Colonels in England, the conscientious objectors, the troops in the trenches, the stretcher bearers and medics etc. Each video should be short and shown to the other groups in a presentation. If video is not available then the drama can be performed live. Each presenting group can then be interviewed by the rest with questions that have been prepared during the research time and are asked from the point of view of their characters. It is very effective to use the children who might still find this difficult to be the directors for the video or take on the role of interviewer, questioning the other groups. Both roles are very motivating and fully involve all the pupils.

CHAPTER 7

Teachers Managing Disputes

This chapter presents the thesis that in order to manage disputes the teacher needs to establish a set of Rules for Dealing with Disputes.

These can be made clear to the pupils by having a set of Rules for Sorting out Arguments on a scroll, see photocopiable sheet, figure 7.1, and displaying them on the wall.

- Rule 1: Everyone has a say.
- Rule 2: Everyone to explain what actually happened.
- Rule 3: Checking out what is said.
- Rule 4: Changing what you do next time.

Clearly the idea of Rules and systems, the 'this is what we do here in this class' feeling will already be a routine in the classroom if the exercises in chapters four and five have been carried out. Make it clear at the beginning of your time with a group what you do when there is an argument and lay down your rules. When disputes arise, you can then refer back to your rules briefly as you begin to help them deal with it. This referring back is very helpful as it in itself acts as a de-escalator. It gives a short breathing space for the antagonists to calm down and it ensures that the teacher maintains a controlling role, that is, stating that this is your classroom and this is how it will be done here.

This chapter is about the teacher establishing the rules. To do this teachers need to use some new skills, in particular new language patterns, and in the next chapter we present ways of teaching pupils to put these rules into practice for themselves.

As language is so crucial in this approach to dispute management we explore some of the issues relating to 'talk and language in the classroom'.

Teachers and children talking in the classroom

As mentioned in chapter three, there is a considerable body of research which shows the importance of talk for learning and concept formation (Vygotsky, 1962, 1978; Mercer, 1991; Wells, 1986; Abercrombie, 1978; Barnes, 1976). Again as noted earlier, some teachers who feel under pressure to demonstrae their competence through effective discipline, actively encourage pupils not to talk as a way of maintaining discipline. For both themselves and their managers

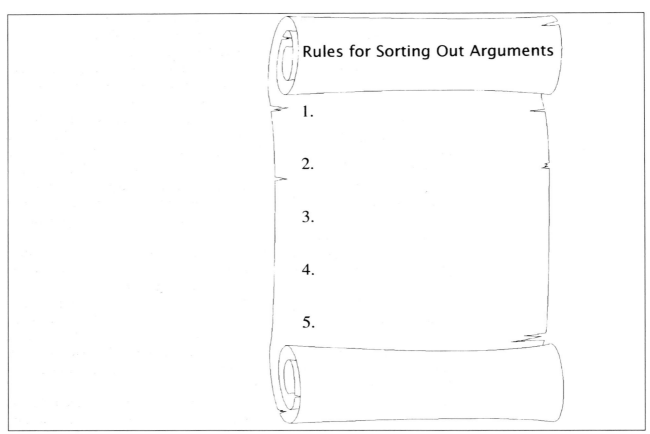

Figure 7.1   Rules for sorting out arguments

a quiet classroom is equated with a good learning environment. The research evidence cited above shows that this is patently untrue. If this 'no noise' rule is a norm in teachers' institutions the authors strongly recommend a staff in-service session to examine its validity. Some schools we work with have developed policies for talk, oracy, or speaking and listening. This is sometimes easier to implement in schools where the issue of English not being a mother tongue or first language is high on the agenda.

Analysis of the amount of talk that pupils and adults use in the classroom demonstrates that teachers do the majority of the talking and pupils do very little. Flanders (1970) found as a result of detailed observations, that in any lesson two thirds of any activity in a classroom was talk and two thirds of that was teacher talk. This imbalance is also compounded by the number of pupils in the class. It means that some pupils will speak very little throughout the day, perhaps only one or two minutes.

In terms of the type of talk that has been observed, Sarah Tann (1988) noted that even when children in the primary setting are organised in groups around tables, they continue to work as individuals, rarely talking about their work. It would seem that the children still believe that school work is what you do alone and they do not see new seating arrangements as changing that. This message is given to the children through the 'don't copy' instruction. The stress is on individualised assessment tasks which inevitably discourages talk about work. This means that talk will be for social interaction and there is a strong likelihood that talk of this nature will be perceived by teachers as off task, talking out of turn. In order for children's language to be fully used to aid their learning the message given out by the teacher must change.

Pupils' classroom language not surprisingly follows the same pattern. They talk to maintain their personal organisation. Talk is used to ask for a rubber, complain that they have lost a pencil, accuse others of moving their book. The phrases they use are copied from others and as such represent the kind of scripted language mentioned in chapter three. They have well practised scripts for their social maintenance. One particular favourite which ensures a legitimate 'break' from work, is 'Please may I go to the toilet; I'm desperate.' This is accompanied with non-verbal wiggling to indicate just how desperate. This is a successful script to be reused and copied by others. It is a script because they are not saying directly how they feel or what they want, they are using a set of lines to communicate a set of needs.

Maintenance of group control requires other scripts. Pupils maintain their place in the group by using stock phrases such as 'I'll batter you after school,' or 'My brother will sort you out,' or 'Just you wait till later'.

Other less aggressive scripts also function to maintain children's place in a group. These are often in the form of put downs to others such as 'You always make a mess don't you' or 'Spellings easy, why can't you spell?' Such phrases are common parlance in a classroom and indicative of a group where competing for your place is vital. Other scripts are used to reprimand and praise other children. However our observations show that reprimand or complaint is frequently heard whilst praise for a peer is very rare. These scripts are more usually used to 'tell on someone' to the teacher. Most teachers are familiar with the list of common complaints about copying, moving chairs, not sharing books, etc. The scripts are so similar for many children that the teacher often ceases to take any notice of any of the repeated complaints however well founded.

Finally, children have scripts to deal with the question and answer sessions with the teacher. They learn to answer 'outguess the teacher' questions where they try to match what they say as nearly as possible with the teacher's ideal model answer. They very rarely have scripts for teaching each other new concepts, discussing new ideas, debating etc.

Pupils' classroom talk reflects the model of teachers' talk. If asked, most teachers would say they talk to teach new ideas. In fact a large proportion of their talk is low level organisational instructions, maintenance of group control, individual praise and reprimand, conducting question and answer sessions; very little is actual explanation of new concepts. Teachers we have worked with have checked this out by tape recording themselves and analysing their own talk. They have been both depressed and horrified to find that their own results have echoed our previous statements about type of teacher talk.

Talking out of turn as disruptive behaviour

The authors believe that many children who talk out of turn do so because they have learnt this script and it has for them a pay-off. Attention from the teacher is a likely pay-off, also feelings of worth because you are being attended to, exploration and refinement of personal ideas through vocalising them, positive feedback from peers through admiration of ideas expressed, and hearing the sound of your own voice as a way of establishing your place in a large group.

This list could equally well apply to the teachers' talk.

Talk in the classroom takes on great importance when disruptive behaviour is the issue. Disruptive behaviour is not only demonstrated through what the pupils say, but how they say it and when they say it. Talking out of turn as previously noted is the single most cited behaviour that teachers can identify when asked what behaviour most disrupts the classroom. Not only is literally talking out of turn disruptive but swearing, shouting, being verbally abusive, muttering under the breath, being 'cheeky' or rude, having the last word, are all aspects of talking out of turn. Dealing with this sort of disruption then becomes a verbal battle which teachers find exhausting and are destined never to win. An exercise we have found useful is to involve the pupils themselves in recording the amount of TOOT (Talking Out Of Turn). The spotters checklist for this is showing in figure 7.2.

Changing teacher scripts

As with the other skills presented in this book, the most effective way to change pupil scripts is to change the model the teacher presents first. The benefits are that:

- the pupils then know what the teacher is talking about when they teach it;
- the pupils have seen it in action and seen it work;
- given that the pupils have learned some of their old behaviours by copying the teacher, modelling must be a powerful teaching tool.

Teacher skill: broken record technique

There are two important elements to using the broken record.

One is to state and then repeat your need, which is usually a behavioural statement, without blame or escalation and the second is to ensure that the other person knows you are listening to them.

Cutting out any blame in your statement is very hard to do and involves a very careful examination of what exactly is being said. 'Why did you do that?' may look blameless but it assumes guilt (they did it) and motive (they had a reason).

Therefore teachers need to practice using blame-free statements in everyday situations so that the skill is there for them when there is a crisis:

'John do you know what happened to the scissors? I saw you using them and I can't find them, can you help me?'

Claire, do you know how these crisps got split on the tutor room floor, it's a bit of a mess isn't it? Can you help me find out what happened?

The broken record techniques is where you repeat what it is that you want the child to do *without adding new demands*. Often when we feel pressured we act as children do in demanding more and more until our demands could never be met. 'Stop that', 'Stop that this minute', 'Stop that and sit down', 'You stop that and come and sit down here', 'Stop that and sit down quietly and stop that

Spotter's Check Sheet for TOOT

Type of activity	Teacher introducing the lesson	Working individually	Working with a partner	Working in a group	Whole class circle
Name of Pupil 1					
Name of Pupil 2					
Name of Pupil 3					
Name of Pupil 4					

Figure 7.2 Spotter's check sheet for TOOT. TOOT is short for talking out of turn: silly noises, interruptions, shouting out and whispering are all examples of talking out of turn. Put a tally mark each time your pupil TOOTs during each activity. Use this spotter sheet to talk about the effect of talking out of turn on you and on the class.

99

crying noise.' etc. An ever escalating list of demands. The broken record suggests that teachers reword this script in two ways, firstly, as an 'I' statement, i.e. 'I need you to stop and sit down' and to stick to that without adding to it. They also have to convey to the student that they have heard them, so the teacher repeats the student's demands, objections, viewpoints and then re-asserts their own demands.

Again this needs to be practised in everyday situations first.

'Sit down and make a badge, yes I know that you would rather do lego but I want you to sit down and make a badge.'

was used with year six children.

'I want you to discuss the three most important factors in your choice for the site of the dam, no do not write anything, I want you to discuss three points first, no, do not get your pens out, just discuss the three points, yes three points everyone please, in a discussion.'

was used with year ten students for geography. Relying on statement of need and using the broken record technique is part of the recommended way of Assertive Discipline (Lee Canter, 1976).

Teacher Skill: hearing both sides of the argument

As mentioned previously there is a tendency for teachers to make assumptions about pupils' behaviour and motivations, often based upon little evidence and lots of reputation. This is particularly noticeable in assemblies. In the classroom the following interchange has been observed.

The teacher notices a pupil who appears to be behaving aggressively. If the pupil is normally not aggressive the teacher says, 'Jo, what on earth has happened to upset you like this?' If however the pupil is one who has often been aggressive the teacher says, 'Josh, I might have known there would be trouble near you, stop that at once.'

For children with emotional and behavioural difficulties this might compound their problems. There is little point in changing your behaviour when you get the blame anyway. The cry, 'Everyone is picking on me' is not always an empty one.

It is helpful if teachers set a rule that says they will listen to disruptive children to give their side of the story.

For example, 'Mike, you seem to have just…' or 'Can you tell me what has just happened? and describe what they are just supposed to have done. 'Is that right or not?'. Then listen carefully to the explanation using parroting throughout to ensure that both you and they are clear about what they are saying. At the end it is also helpful to paraphrase. Note the use of the pupil's name. This helps the pupil to assimilate what is being said rather than dismissing it. It is helpful to encourage pupils to use each other's names as well.

Pupil skill: checking out to see if it was an accident

When this is a dispute between children, make it clear that you wish them to do the same. Allow them to role play the alternative. For example, consider an incident where Heather puts the chair on Catherine's foot, Catherine then hits

Heather who goes to the teacher to complain that she has been hit for no reason. The role play can practice the two girls saying to each other;

'Heather, when you went over to the rubbish bin you put your chair on my foot and hurt it. It seemed to me that you did it on purpose. Is that what happened?'

This gives Heather the opportunity either to say sorry or to demonstrate that she clearly didn't know what she had done or that although she knew, it was misinterpreted and not on purpose. If, however she really did mean it, then the question opens up the door for her to say what her reason was. This is the three part message being taught to pupils, in order that they can check out to see if something is an accident or not.

Dealing with disputes

One of the most common occurrences leading to 'disruption' is the eruption of a dispute between two or more pupils. Very often the first indication to the teacher that there is something amiss is when the first physical blow is landed. By this time the teacher is confronted with very emotional pupils who have already become entrenched in their positions, (figure 7.3). Tempers are high and pupils unlikely to respond to reasonable tones by the teacher. The teacher usually raises her voice above the noise to regain control, to order the children to stop and then to separate and remove the pupil seen striking the blow. The result is temporary calm but our experience, in common with many teachers', is that this erupts again, usually after school when one pupil waits for another, often having recruited reinforcements in the meantime. The trouble then comes back threefold and both the pupils and the teacher are in a lose-lose situation.

Changing the teacher's script to one which is more likely to have a win-win outcome takes time to learn and practice. Whilst we here outline a step by step approach, teachers will find that they are dealing with all aspects at all times and may need to call on more than one of the steps, even if they have not yet practised them.

Figure 7.3   When the first blow lands

Step One – initial defusing

Often the crucial time in dealing with a dispute is the initial two or three minutes. This is the time when tempers are hottest and emotions are making all those involved deaf. This is when the broken record is at its most effective because it has the effect of calming pupils down and allowing everyone to get to the point where the incident can be unravelled.

To diffuse the initial situation, use the broken record technique. The rules that can be established based on the broken record technique are:

- No blame – innocent until proven guilty.
- I hear you (repeat back what they have just said) and I need…(state your own demand).

When tempers are frayed it is very important to make sure that you can be heard. Teachers, historically, have used loud and vibrant tones to do that. Resulting behavioural problems for children habitually shouted at in the home and at school are well known by many teachers – the shutting off, the upward turned eyes, the drooping shoulders, the don't care stance, the runners etc. The authors advocate a different approach to getting your voice heard, that is, repeating back what the child has said, or if they have not said anything then observing their physical posture and using feedback on the emotion it displays.

The teacher's script using the broken record for a dispute between Jamie and Gary might look this:

> I can see you are very angry and tense but I need you to stop and come and sit down.
>
> You seem to be very upset by what has happened and I need you to stop and come and sit down.
>
> So Gary has hit you has he? Well I need you to stop and come and sit down.
>
> You feel that everyone is picking on you, not just Gary, but I need you to stop and come and sit down.

The reader might feel that this could never work with their pupils. We would recommend that they try it. The authors' experience is that time and time again, without ever a failure, it has worked with even the most difficult of pupils and at the top end of the age range. In fact one of the authors began her teaching with 'disaffected' year nine and ten students, and this approach was the only strategy that did work. The more difficult the pupil the longer you will need to continue to repeat. You might guess the pupil's comments in the above script. What is important is that even if the pupil is swearing and shouting and physically destructive, the teacher should keep reacting in the same way and not get drawn in and emotionally charged by the pupil script.

Step Two – unravelling what actually happened

Establish that what you are now going to do is to go through the rules. Remind the pupils of your rules.

Rule 1. Everyone has a say.

Everyone will get a chance to say what their point of view is. Emphasise the implications of this rule, as it means that since all points of view will be listened to there will be no need to interrupt the other person.

Be very systematic in the way you ask for each version of events and allow no interruptions at all, reminding anyone who speaks that they will get their own uninterrupted turn.

If possible, ensure that the students are heard in a clear order, i.e. left to right in a line so that there is clear turn taking with no chance of anyone being left out and no chance of being chosen to be first or last indicating anything about the importance of what you have to say.

Rule 2. Everyone to say what actually happened.

Include all protagonists and eye witnesses. Dismiss any hearsay witnesses as their view does not help to describe the actual events but only reinforces assumptions. When everyone has had their turn, offer the chance to all those involved to add any further information.

Finally offer everyone the opportunity to question and clarify what any other has said. It is important that it is made clear that each view is valid and has something to add to the whole picture. Each person can be invited to take their turn with a phrase such as 'What information do you have about what happened?', 'Tell me what happened from your point of view', 'That is what John felt happened, what do you feel happened?'

With younger children it helps to explain at the outset that you are dealing with a jigsaw and they all have some pieces to fit in. This visual image helps them to see it as a co-operative venture, not one that involves blaming.

Rule 3. Checking out what is said.

The mistake many of us make when listening to an account of what has happened is to overlay what we are hearing with the history of events in the past. This encourages assumptions about motives and deeds, especially where children have a reputation for a particular behaviour. The best way to ensure that this does not happen, and that each new incident gets a fresh sheet, is to systematically check out what is said by reporting back what you think that person has said, (figure 7.4).

There are many reasons for doing this. Firstly, it ensures that all present feel that you are really listening and so it makes it worth while disclosing information to you. It also has the added advantage of helping you to actually hear what is being said, not what you think might have happened from your own viewpoint. It helps to slow down the person doing the telling and gives them thinking time to ensure that their account is as accurate as possible and includes the detail which is usually the key to the incident. Try doing this every few sentences, the phrase 'So you are saying that...' is a helpful one to begin each repeat. The overall effect of repeating is to clarify for everyone what happened and to ensure that the protagonists begin to hear the other point of view.

The model to the children is very clear. You have not just said everyone will be heard but you have ensured that everyone feels as if they were heard, and not just by the teacher.

Rule 4. Changing what you do next time.

Our experience of using the Rules for Disputes is that they usually conclude with a realisation that the dispute arose from mistaken identity, miscommunication, jumping to conclusions or assumptions about another person's motives. Awareness of these factors being the cause results in all parties being happy that the difference is resolved. When everyone has disclosed their view, a recap of what happened and what went wrong can be summarised by the teacher. The teacher might ask for suggestions as to what went wrong and what could have been done to prevent it. It is a good idea to allow the pupil who has committed the 'misdeed' to make the first suggestion but allow others to give their ideas too.

Figure 7.4   Checking out what was said

Again, the teacher's role is to repeat these ideas and summarise the courses of action open to the pupils at each point in the dispute, based on their own ideas.

The object of this is not to punish wrong doing but to stop it repeating itself over and over again. The pupil needs to build up a variety of responses to the same situation so that next time, and there will usually be a next time, they can try a different response that has been suggested and get a different outcome. For pupils deeply entrenched in a particular script it is often worth taking time with this group of children to rehearse one of the other responses suggested. Trying it out loud with the people who were involved is very powerful for many pupils and although it might feel very false when they do it they find it easier the next time it happens.

Asking the other pupils to give their opinion on whether that sounded better, would have made them act differently, made them less angry or hurt, is also helpful in getting behavioural change, as it represents positive peer feedback.

The anger being displayed might well be related to historical incidents which have never been really resolved and resentments which can fester and grow into enormous size. Time taken to find out historical as well as immediate cause can be a good investment, especially where the pupil habitually behaves in an aggressive or disruptive way.

It can be seen from the above description that dealing with disputes this way is very time consuming. Indeed it constitutes the caseload of form tutors, pastoral year heads, and pastoral deputies.

The experience of all of our teachers and students who have adopted our Rules Approach is that although it is time consuming in the beginning the more times they go through the process, the less time it takes. Also the pupils themselves respond more quickly so it is more effective at getting to the root of the problem. Where this does differ from traditional teacher driven punishment and sanction systems is that this method changes children's behaviour. That in itself quickly begins to recoup the time spent initially as there are fewer and fewer disputes to sort out.

CHAPTER 8

Changing Pupils' Scripts

Old scripts

Teacher skill: modelling new scripts

As raised in chapter two, all of us have ways of saying things that we have learned throughout our lives: our phraseology, our accent, our vocabulary. We also learn particular scripts which we use in certain circumstances. For example, we may have learned how to complain about shoddy service in a restaurant with successful results, so whenever we need to complain we will use a similar script to the one that we have used in the past. We also have learned scripts from our parents which are not as successful. When we become mothers and fathers ourselves we find ourselves using phrases and indeed whole conversations which are repeats of those which our parents had with us. This is so, even if we promised ourselves that we would 'never say that to our children', because we hated them so much ourselves.

These 'repeats' are known in transactional analysis as 'scripts'. Some scripts are helpful to us whilst others lock us into a conversation which repeatedly has a negative outcome. Scripts are used particularly at times of stress where the emotional level of the situation seems to make us call up old reserves, even if they have failed us in the past. Students with emotional and behavioural difficulties have also become locked into these negative scripts. Trigger phrases used by parents, teachers or peers set them on a script which repeatedly fails to meet their long term needs. With such pupils, teachers need to allow them to explore their present scripts, examine their usefulness and discard those which have negative outcomes.

In order to discard a script all of us need to have a new script with which to replace the old, otherwise it is natural to use the old phrases all over again. Most teachers have probably thought at times, 'If only I'd said…' After the event we can think of a hundred witty replies, assertive responses, pleasant anecdotes. At the time however, we found old, tired phrases leaping out of our mouths, therefore the new script will only be used if it has been practised prior to the situation so that it is more readily available when the brain is busy worrying about emotions.

We suggest in this chapter that pupils with emotional and behavioural difficulties have accumulated a vast number of unhelpful scripts which are continually giving them negative outcomes. However, scripts were not born into us, they were learned and so they can be relearned. These pupils, as do all pupils, need to have many more positive scripts. Learning how to ask for help and offer help (chapter nine), check out rules (chapter five), express feelings (chapter six) and build relationships (chapters four, five and nine) are all scripts which are addressed in other chapters of this book. For those children who have emotional and behavioural problems a script which helps them to sort out their own personal arguments in an effective way is the one explored in this chapter. The methods by which this new script is taught are also relevant for the teaching of any other new script.

When teaching pupils new scripts the work previously done with them on forming a set of rules will prove very helpful, as learning a new script is like learning a new set of rules for what you say and how you say it. The 'Rules for Disputes' established in chapter seven will become the basis for the script learned by the pupils. Each step will need to be taught separately and to all the students. If the child who has most difficulty is struggling to change their script against a tide of old, tired scripts used towards them by the other students then they are far more likely to fail. They will be far more likely to succeed with the support of their peer group, who unfortunately might be finding this task just as difficult themselves.

Steps to making changes

- Model the skills in action

The first step in changing the scripts of pupils who constantly use unsuccessful scripts is for the teacher to change their scripts. For the teacher, powerful in the eyes of all pupils, is their ideal model. As stressed above, an important part of the model is for the teacher to explain what it is that they are doing, their ground rules for dealing with disputes. For youngsters with emotional and behavioural difficulties this gives clear expectations and limits to acceptable behaviour but more than that, begins to introduce a structure which they too can follow.

- Teach the skills

Secondly, and very importantly, the pupils need to be specifically taught the skills that they need to deal with each other using a small steps approach.

- Opportunities for practising the skills

When the skills have been taught they need to be given opportunities to practice and refine them within the classroom as part of the taught curriculum.

- Praise and positive feedback when skills are used

When the pupils feel more confident in using these skills they will be more able to transfer them to the everyday real situations in which they find themselves. Throughout, the power of the teacher's approval and praise can be used to highlight when the skills are used and encourage them in a wider variety of situations.

One child, not uncommonly, used the script 'He did it first' to the extent that it was totally meaningless. In the end it did not relate to a real event, it was no longer even an excuse or defence, it was merely a knee jerk reaction to any questioning of behaviour. For instance, in order to establish whether there were any spare bottles of milk Richard was asked if he had had his milk. He replied, 'Mark had his first' believing the question to be an accusation. To teach Richard a new script when this was so entrenched took a great deal of time, and in fact, even after the new script was established, when he was stressed the old one was still sometimes used. However, it was possible to replace the phrase with other, more helpful scripts.

This was done by the teacher modelling non-accusing questions and accepting all answers in a non-judgmental way, by teaching all the children in the class to use more assertive/adult responses as further models, and by not accepting the old phrase but making Richard rehearse new phrases when the need arose. These phrases were openly suggested by the teacher and other children. The teacher said, 'When you say that he did it first, I feel that you are not really listening to my question and I begin to get cross with you. Please try to say…' or 'What do you think would sound better, Dean?'

Observing behaviour
Pupil skill: recognizing non-verbal cues

Video can be used very effectively for this activity so select or record a two minute incident for children to observe. If video is not available ask a small group to role play an incident.

Divide the class into threes using cards. On each card indicate one of three different roles: those who will listen, those who will watch and those who will watch and listen. Place the listeners behind the television so they cannot see the picture; the watchers to put their own fingers in their ears so they cannot listen and allow the other group to both watch and listen. Each person should then write down or draw what they thought was happening and particularly who they thought was at fault.

Ask the group to then form their three to discuss what they thought was happening in the clip, referring to what they have written. The watcher and the listener should go first. In their threes ask the pupils to note the differences in their interpretation of what happened. Join two threes to make a six and compare the interpretations. As a six, record the difficulties found in witnessing incidents. Debrief as a whole class.

Describing the behaviour – lessening the assumptions
Pupil skill: Observing and describing behaviour

Following the video exercise, divide the children into random threes. Pair up the threes. Each three is to decide on three 'mini dramas' which they are going to mime. These ideally should be playground or classroom incidents. Each group should then perform their mimes for the other group who write down what they think is happening. Before the sixes talk to each other about what they were miming or what they thought was happening the teacher should give some examples of what is meant by 'describing the behaviour'. This description of the behaviour is referred to in chapter 6. The skill is difficult for teachers, so be prepared for pupils to find it equally tricky at first. Prompts, like 'So what did he actually do/say?' are useful.

Ask each group to repeat each mime while the other group try to describe exactly the behaviour and record their observations. The six pupils should then join together and take it in turns to each talk about one mime and their two records. First the impression, then the behavioural description, checking out with the opposite 'team' the accuracy of each. What children will notice is that when you check out your first impression by actually describing what you saw rather than what you assumed was going on, you might confirm your first impression, but you might instead get a very different picture.

Checking out assumptions

Teacher skill: Role play
Pupil skill: observing and describing behaviour

This exercise follows on from the pupils looking at describing the behaviour and one way of checking out their assumptions. It encourages them to see that you can actually check out assumptions face to face with the person.

One reason children and older students often have disputes is because they mishear and/or misunderstand something that is said, or they believe the tales told second or third hand by a 'friend'. If you wish to change the normal script of 'Miss, John said that Jiva said I'm smelly, tell him Miss,' to a less wearing one, another 'checking out script' needs to be learned. This can ensure a more accurate picture of what one pupil believes another pupil might have done.

Role play is the best vehicle for learning new scripts as it allows pupils to imagine the other protagonists in their dispute. Whilst pupils usually enjoy role play it must be stressed that this exercise calls upon an advanced stage of the pupil's skills, and if it is attempted prior to other skills being learned it is likely to be less effective.

The role play groups should contain five members, who are best selected randomly. Use cards which are differently numbered 1-5. Roles are to be attributed to the numbered card holders.

1 – Director
2 – Script Editor
3 – 'You' on the script cards
4 – 'Other child' on the script cards
5 – Bystander, witness or friend

Each director should be given one of the script cards, which can be photocopied from the sheet provided, figure 8.1. The director should then explain the situation to the actors and they should act out the drama bringing the incident to its most likely conclusion.

The director should then question the characters about their motivation, their feelings and their assumptions about each other. Based upon these questions the group should then discuss the motivation of the protagonists and the outcome they have enacted. As a group, they should list other different possible motivations for each character and decide which motivation they are going to try out. Only then should they re run the drama.

The teacher should put the three possible motivations on a large chart or board and explain:

- negative – i.e. on purpose, to get back at you, to upset you, feud.
- neutral – i.e. an accident, didn't know or realise.
- positive – intended to be helpful, thought that you wanted or knew.

The script editor should make a note of the main changes in what people actually say. This can be repeated a number of times with the director noting the changes in emotional levels, voices, gestures etc. These can be recorded on copies of the Drama Record provided, figure 8.2.

Finally the group should look at the observations made and try to draw some conclusions about what was happening, and be prepared to share their findings with the whole class.

> You have just come in from dinner and gone to get your bag. You see the other child standing by the coat pegs with your pencil case in his/her hand. Do you think he is stealing?

> You see the other child with a picture that you have drawn in their hand. It is all screwed up. Do you think he/she has done this to your picture?

> You are sitting bent over and concentrating on your work. Suddenly your chair tips up under you and you fall off, banging your chin on the table. You turn around and see the other child just behind your chair. Do you suspect he/she tipped you up?

> In the playground you are playing football with a group of friends and another group move in on the game. A couple of kicks later, your ball suddenly deflates. You are very angry about the ruined ball. Do you think this was what they wanted to happen?

> You help to run the school tuck shop and you have been put on duty with a new person whom you don't know. At the end of the tuck shop there is some money missing from the cash box. It has never happened before. Do you think that the new boy/girl has got anything to do with the missing money?

> You are walking across the playground with a friend when you see a group of the older children, known for being aggressive, crowding around your younger brother. He is crying. You go over. What do you think has been happening?

Figure 8.1   Role play script cards

Take 1. / Take 2.
(Delete as appropriate)

Character	Motivation	Emotion	Gesture	Voice	Words used
You					
Other					
Bystander					

Figure 8.2 Drama record: script card incident

111

The teacher can then write up a script and ask the children to insert that in the drama, at an appropriate point.

WHEN I SAW YOU .... I THOUGHT THAT ....
IS THAT RIGHT?

If any group is having difficulty, the teacher might wish to help the group by introducing the visual image of a video being replayed. Some children find this very useful. The teacher can ask them to go back in the conversation (or argument) and then stop them at each point in order for them to try the checking out process with phrases such as, 'So you think Tina meant... Ask her if that is what she meant.' Liberal praise for using the checking out script should be given.

On and under chairs – using the broken record

Teacher skill: Modelling broken record
Pupil skills: Using broken record

Teaching the pupils to use the broken record technique gives them a very powerful skill to use, particularly in a crisis. Also pupils knowing the technique does not stop it working on them when the teacher uses it... The following activity is a very good way of teaching the technique to both adults and pupils.

First divide the pupils into random pairs and give them a letter A or B. Using a guided fantasy, a 'Feeling' dice circle or just talking about an imaginary situation, allow them to remember a time when they were angry or upset. Give each pair a chair and ask A to either stand on or crawl under the chair, whichever they would most feel like doing when upset. B then should try to talk them down or out from under the chair. When all pupils have been persuaded allow them to talk about what it was the person said or did that made them change from hiding and being upset to coming out. The class should list as many of these as they can.

The teacher should then demonstrate the most simple broken record technique with a volunteer child, where the teacher just keeps on saying that they want them to come down/out. With a second volunteer the teacher should then demonstrate the broken record technique using a two part message, 'I can hear/see you are angry/upset but I want you to come down/out.' The volunteers can then talk about how that felt. The pairs can then try this out for themselves, with B now standing on or hiding under the chair and A using the broken record to get them down.

As a way of practising the technique, ask the children to think of other situations in which they think this technique might help to calm someone down, then let the pupils act them out.

Practising an apology

Pupil skill: Negotiation when the emotional content is high

Some children do find it very difficult to apologise for an accidental injury caused to another, simply because being made to apologise has been used in the past as a way to demonstrate that they have been defeated. They might indeed feel sorry for an action, but whilst an apology is regarded as some sort of salve for a situation it will remain a climb down to be avoided. However, as mentioned in the previous chapter, many quite fearsome fights could have been avoided if the person who accidentally caused someone some problem had immediately apologised and explained.

One way to address this business of offering an immediate apology for a true accidental injury is to organise the pupils into small groups and ask them to draw a strip cartoon of a recent remembered incident where they either felt aggrieved or where they hurt someone or broke something by mistake. Having drawn the initial picture they should draw two endings. One where the person apologises before they are accused and the result; and one where they wait until the incident develops until they apologise. The group should be asked to discuss and draw their own conclusions.

Devising a new script. Three part message

Teacher skill: role play, structuring steps, prompting
Pupil skills: Using a three part message

This is a difficult skill so we recommend that the pupils have an opportunity to practice using the worksheet provided (figure 8.3) using an imaginary incident first. They can either use scenarios provided by the teacher or they can make up their own, as shown in this book. They should talk through the scenario and imagine the outcomes and record that on the worksheet. Working in a pair or small group they should then try to think about the actual words that are likely to be used in these circumstances. The words are likely to reflect a combination of incidents remembered by the group. The teacher should then explain the three part message as described in chapter two:

- describing the actual behaviour;
- saying how you feel because of the behaviour;
- describing the result.

The children can then try to think of the best three part message to convey their feelings in their scenario. They might then try acting out the scenario first without and then with the three part message. An important part of this activity is for the teacher to ensure that the pupils talk about the difference in their feelings when using this script, as some will initially feel awkward and the language will feel clumsy. They need to share this so that everyone will know it is not just them.

Teaching the three part message with a real incident

Teacher skills: structuring steps, prompting
Pupil skills: negotiation when the emotional content is high

Teachers can again use any of the previously mentioned methods to encourage their pupils to think about a time when there was an incident where they experienced a bad outcome. It might be an incident that seems to repeat itself often, for a particular pupil. Use random pairs for them to tell their partner

Changing the Script.

Think of a recent incident when you have argued with someone and fallen out. Draw a cartoon picture showing what happened in the beginning.

Write what the other person said to you in this speech bubble.

Write what you said to them in this speech bubble.

Now draw what happened at the end of your argument.

Next time try using a new script. When you have tried it out in a role play try it out for real. Write what your new script could be here.

....(name) ,

when you ....
(tell them what they did)

I feel ....
(tell them how it made you feel)

and so I ....
(tell them what it makes you want to do).

Next time you have an argument, try this out. Make a note of what happens as a result.

Figure 8.3   Changing the script

114

about such an incident. Their partner should use their active listening skills. The listener's role is to do the following things:

- Listen for the feelings behind the words used and check them out with the speaker using phrases like 'So it makes you feel angry/hurt?'
- Ask their partner to describe the actual behaviour of the other person, not the assumed motive. The actual words used are very important too.

Using the worksheet provided, ask the pairs to record the incident and its outcomes, based upon what was said, with the help of the partner's listening skills.

Finally, rewrite the script section using the feeling and the description of behaviour as well as the result of the incident. The talker can now practise the new script on their listener to see how it sounds and amend it if necessary.

When this is completed the whole exercise can be repeated for the other partner.

When both partners have a new script they should try role playing both with their partner as the other character in the incident.

The Arbiter's Role

Pupil Skills: Negotiating when the emotional content is high

Divide the pupils into random groups of four or five. Ask them to brainstorm the rules for sorting out or managing arguments. If the teacher has been modelling the recommendations in earlier chapters then this should produce a common list for all groups. These rules can then be recorded by the group using their own language on the blank worksheet provided. This blank worksheet should be used at the beginning of this exercise to allow all the children to recap on the rules for disputes to ensure that all the pupils are clear on how they are expected to manage this themselves.

The children's scenarios written and illustrated here should be given out to random groups or the children could write their own. One of the group should be given the role of arbiter, (figure 8.4). The photograph shows one such arbiter at work. Their job is going to be to work like the teacher in trying to reduce the crisis using the broken record. They need to unpick the incident using the five rules, and ensure that they come to a satisfactory conclusion where everyone in the group is left feeling OK.

Teacher praise for Arbiters
Teacher Skill: Giving positive feedback

As we have stressed, teacher praise is a very powerful tool that can be used in encouraging one sort of behaviour over another. Teacher praise can be used to encourage pupils to take on the skilled role of arbiter in their peers' disputes.

When pupils finally come to this stage in using the skills they will have begun to use them in real life situations. When this occurs pupils can be encouraged to tell the teacher, not about the argument or the incident but about the person who was skilled at sorting it out. Teachers report to us, and our own experience supports this, that when the pupils are using these skills the first thing they

Figure 8.4   The Arbiter at work

know about an argument is when it is over. At first, teachers may need to give a certain amount of time for pupils whom they notice trying to sort other children out, and for a while give it priority over the curriculum delivery. This time is well invested, for pupils then become far more able to pay attention to the curriculum as and when it is taught. They are no longer in an emotional state over who said what to them at break and who is going to 'batter them' on the way home.

CHAPTER 9

The Importance of Friendship and Building Positive Peer Relationships

Teachers have reported that when they work in the way outlined in this book with all the pupils in their class then the pupils are more able to build positive relationships and quarrel less. The structures used to teach the skills are also of benefit for delivering the curriculum, especially where bodies of knowledge need to be taught. The benefit for teachers is that more and more of their time is spent teaching and far less in sorting out personal disputes between children. It is also reported that the noise level falls as both the children's and the teacher's emotional pitch drops.

Problems with friendships are readily identified by many secondary teachers, tutors and year heads as the kind of difficulty they spend much valuable time sorting out. Pupils with emotional and behavioural difficulties have particular problems with friends. The chance of them being included and helped by their peers will be increased if their peers are also skilful.

This final chapter seeks to look at the issue of relationships and friendship with peers in particular, and the ways in which the problems some of the children with emotional and behavioural difficulties have with friendships can be overcome.

The effect of friendship on the self-esteem

Research into levels of self-esteem and friendship (Coopersmith, 1967) showed that the regard of the peer group was important to the development of self-esteem. It was shown that those children who had a 'best friend' had a higher self-esteem than those who did not. (Sullivan, 1953). As pupils with emotional and behavioural problems have a lower self-esteem than their peer group (Lund, 1988) the effect of having a friend takes on great significance.

Pupils who are behaving in an unacceptable way in school may be those who are also finding relationships with their peers difficult. The increasing poor feedback diminishes their self-esteem. As previously outlined, as their feelings of self worth fall then these pupils seem to respond by behaving in any way that awards them the notice of their teachers, their parents or their peers. This might give them the temporary accolades of their peers but these 'friends' soon get tired of being tarred with the same brush.

Such pupils drift from friend to friend, with many of their relationships ending badly. When a friend 'goes off' then there is a great deal of hurt felt and that hurt is defended by either blaming another child for taking them away, or projecting onto the ex-friend all the disliked qualities in the child themselves, or sometimes by engineering actual physical fights in which they can 'fall out' without further damage to the self-esteem. As we have seen with many behaviours in school, these strategies are actually defence mechanisms, protecting the youngster from the pain of being deserted.

As they use these defence mechanisms over and over again the pupils with whom they have argued become reluctant to reform the friendship. Other students witness the behaviour and do not wish to be the next in this long line of apparent victims. All the while these children are adding to their self image as someone that no one wants to know. In some cases their desperation for a friend becomes a frenzy of dares, trying to impress their peers. Such pupils can be used very easily by the peer group to carry out very dangerous and very entertaining feats.

Figure 9.1   Being protected from the pain of being alone

In earlier chapters we have discussed the influence of teacher expectations and assumptions about children based upon knowledge about their social class, medical condition and intelligence. The same is the case for the peer group. Assumptions about other pupils are first based upon an initial impression. This is usually physical. Kirkpatrick and Sanders (1978) found that children sat next to those with an athletic body shape whilst fat and skinny pupils were avoided. There is a clear message to those pupils about whether or not they are liked. Lawson (1980), showed that many initial judgements were based upon the body image alone and that these body shapes were seen to associate with many other traits. These messages from student to student are very important and very subtle. Indeed, Kirchner and Vondraek (1975) found that when children were asked to score themselves on a 'Who likes you' scale the role of the peers and siblings was immense, being far more influential than that of the parents or the teachers.

If this first impression is then reinforced by witnessing 'undesirable' behaviour then a negative relationship is likely. If further negative information is received about social background, intelligence or, on some estates, the family, then further assumptions are made. As with the teachers, these are value judgements based upon the pupil's own background. If no other information of a positive nature is available about the child then there will continue to be a negative relationship between the children.

Figure 9.2   Pupils need structures for getting to know each other

Teachers, when structuring their classroom and curriculum, need to bear in mind this research. Pupils need to be helped to get to know each other, beyond the first impression, and beyond the defensive mask that so many of them are wearing to protect their self-esteem. We have early discussed the usefulness of random pairs and fours in allowing children to work together for safe, short periods of time, within a clear structure. These structures, and those of whole circles and carousels allow all children to get more information about each other and find common interests.

Many teachers will be familiar with 'the unholy alliance' that is two children who are unable to form positive friendships with other children teaming up together. When both of these children are displaying difficult behaviour in school this fills many teachers with horror. Their subsequent misdeeds might lead any teacher to conclude that they must be split up as they are making each other worse. This is not in fact the case. The research on friendships and self-esteem would support the view that the friendship might be encouraging bad behaviour initially but the friendship itself could be of benefit to the self-esteem of both pupils. There is however a BUT! Unless the pupils are taught the skills to be friends, even the most unholy of alliances will break down, with further damage to the self-esteem. Past scripts and behaviour patterns will intervene, probably before the teacher does. Rather than work against such friendships, teachers could find better results by using that relationship as a basis for work on friendships skills with that pair of pupils.

Skills training for the whole class

Teacher skill: Identifying friendship skills.

Pupils with emotional and behavioural difficulties need to have friends just as all pupils need friends, that is, they need to feel liked and special and to belong. Pupils with emotional and behavioural difficulties need friends desperately. If, however, a downward spiral of low self-esteem and poor behaviour has already developed, the pupil might not have enough friendship skills. Those friendship skills which they do have, they do not or cannot use, perhaps because they have no relationship in which to show them. To help these pupils they need both a friendly relationship and to be taught the skills needed to be a friend.

The teacher, faced with such pupils, and we would argue, all the pupils, needs to teach all the children the skills needed to be a friend. Social training in the past has concentrated on the 'problem' child. However, research into integration clearly demonstrates the importance of all the children being able to be friends with the difficult pupil. When the emotionally and behaviourally difficult pupil is first trying out being friends, they need supportive peers on whom to practice their skills. We are all aware of just how unfriendly the most 'normal' of children can be when they feel threatened by someone whom they perceive as being different to them. These children need to be taught how to be friends with everyone, no matter how odd looking, in order to support the progress made by the child who has the severer problem with relationships.

Friendly Tree

Pupil skills: friendship skills

In fours ask the children to brainstorm the type of things that friends do. That four then joins another four and the eight compile a list of friendly behaviours. In a small circle the children then give examples of the type of action that they mean. This detail will help all the children to come to a better understanding of what they mean by friendly.

Ask each child to describe an example of a personal incident when someone has behaved in one of the friendly ways towards them and how they felt. This process both helps children identify the friendly behaviours and raises their level of understanding of what that means for them personally. Importantly, it helps the pupils identify what effect such behaviours have on the way they feel. This link with the positive emotions produced by friendly deeds is one which many pupils need to have spelled out for them. They often feel badly as a result of a lack of these good emotions but they do not know why they feel bad.

This circle work can be recorded by means of the 'Friendly Tree' where friendly incidents are drawn or written about. For younger children this may need to be enlarged to accommodate pictures. Some classes might want to draw a very large class tree on which all children can record one incident.

If the class has undertaken work on rules as recommended in chapter four then the exercises outlined there can be used to establish 'Rules for Friendship'. You may find that there are similarities between some of these and the rules for the classroom. This is especially true of the 'No put down rule' (See 'put down' and 'push up' worksheet, figure 5.4).

For very damaged children it might be necessary for this one simple rule to be established then practised for some time. This certainly can help to promote the classroom ethos where friendships are possible. However, friendship skills are more than just this and all pupils need to be helped to work towards getting more skilled in their relationships. The first step is to unpick what being a friend actually requires.

Figure 9.3   Friendly tree

What does friendship look like?

Pupils who believe themselves to be of low worth might never have had a positive relationship with a peer friend on which to base their knowledge of what friends do. Without such a model there is little hope of them behaving in that way themselves; they simply do not know how.

Friendship, when described by pupils, is often at first a record of deeds rather

121

Figure 9.4   Apples for hanging on the friendly tree

than behaviours. Teachers need to help children to sort out the deeds from the actual behaviours that make a person appear friendly. Commonly named behaviours are listening to me, sharing with me, choosing me, playing with me, helping me, standing up for me, talking to me, looking after me, and of course there are others.

The 'Friendly Dice' provided (figure 9.5) has been constructed using the behaviours often cited by pupils doing the exercise above but particular groups of pupils may wish to have other behaviours on the dice, and these can be easily made…

The Friendly Dice

Pupil skills: describing friendship skills

Sit the pupils in a circle, and ask them to roll the dice and say when a person was friendly to them in the way that the dice shows. Ask them to describe what happened and how it made them feel. Use teacher praise to encourage detailed descriptions that do not make moral judgements, but do talk about the emotions aroused by the action. The greater the detail the more useful it is to the pupil who has little understanding of how to be friendly.

Pupils can then be asked to follow up their disclosures with designs for a poster advocating being friendly. The poster shows someone doing a friendly action. Similar activities can be speaking onto tape or writing a story of a friendly deed. These stories can be dramatised and if video is available, recorded.

The friendly and unfriendly dice can also be used in small groups. Although this reduces the amount of models a child hears it can increase the details and reduce the time needed for the initial sharing. As with the Feeling Dice a board game can be constructed to aid the pupils to take turns and to disclose their thoughts.

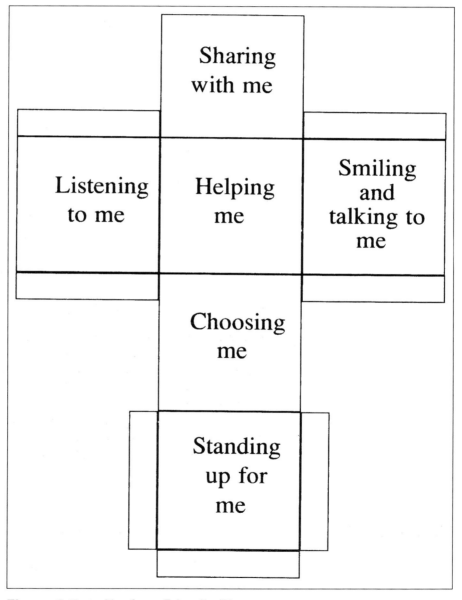

Figure 9.5　　Net for a Friendly Dice

```
┌─────────────────────────────────────────────────────────────┐
│                    ┌──────────┐                              │
│                    │ Taking   │                              │
│                    │   my     │                              │
│                    │  stuff   │                              │
│           ┌────────┼──────────┼────────┐                     │
│           │        │   Not    │        │                     │
│           │Picking │ choosing │        │                     │
│           │  on    │  me and  │Staring │                     │
│           │  me    │ ignoring │  at    │                     │
│           │        │   me     │  me    │                     │
│           └────────┼──────────┼────────┘                     │
│                    │ Copying  │                              │
│                    │ off me   │                              │
│                 ┌──┼──────────┼──┐                           │
│                 │  │Calling me│  │                           │
│                 │  │names and │  │                           │
│                 │  │ talking  │  │                           │
│                 │  │behind my │  │                           │
│                 │  │  back    │  │                           │
│                 └──┴──────────┴──┘                           │
└─────────────────────────────────────────────────────────────┘
```

Figure 9.6   Net for an Unfriendly Dice

Unfriendly Dice

Repeat the whole exercise with the Unfriendly Dice, (figure 9.6), again prompting for details and praising their descriptions without any moral judgements. Similar follow ups can be used but the role plays need more structure than with friendly dice. Common incidents are: picking on me, taking my stuff, ignoring me, leaving me out, calling me names, bullying me, hurting me, staring at me, copying my work, talking about me behind my back.

These are very useful as the nature of the role play allows the children to repeat a disliked unfriendly incident and rewrite the ending. This, like the work in changing the children's scripts, can be salutary as it gives them an alternative way of dealing with an unfriendly incident next time. There are two clear advantages in this. Firstly the child has an alternative behaviour rehearsed, and secondly it can also help children to sort out past feelings of resentment that they may not have been able to deal with before. Many children may in fact, have been unaware of where their negative feelings about another person had come from.

Friendly deeds

Pupil skill: identifying friendship skills; giving positive feedback

This activity must be structured with either a pair, four, circle or carousel in which the children can share their examples. The teacher's or pupils' preferred structure can be chosen, giving further friendly modelling. Teachers should stress that the role of sharing in these structures is for the others to help everyone think about a time when someone was friendly to them. This in itself is a model for what friends do; they help you to think about things that are hard. Having shared their ideas, the Friendly Deeds sheet (figure 9.7) can be used to record what has been remembered. One or two incidents are enough on the first occasion.

These can then be used to record on-going friendly deeds. At the end of a day or two, the pairs or small groups can re-form and share what is now on their sheets. The awareness of their friendly deeds being recorded will always raise the

Friendly Deeds

What friendly things am I doing to others ? This is my honest record.

Date	Name of the person	What exactly I did	How that made me feel

Figure 9.7   Friendly deeds sheet

amount of friendly deeds that are being done by class members. This in itself is important for pupils who need many models before they too can try out what, for them, might be new ways of behaving.

The second friendly deeds sheet (figure 9.8) asks pupils to record the friendly deeds that they do for others. This should be attempted second, preferably during the following few days. Teachers should be using the same format of sharing ideas as in the first. The reason for this is that pupils who have had very little practice in being friendly will have needed to identify what is a friendly act before they can successfully try it for themselves. Following the previous examples, pupils should be able to help each other remember things that they did for each other that were friendly. A whole circle is also a good way of ensuring that all pupils receive the feedback that they have recently done something that is friendly to someone else.

My Friendly Record

Who is doing Friendly things to me ? Write what they did that was friendly.

Date	Name of the person	What exactly they did	How that made me feel

Figure 9.8   Friendly deeds for others

For some classes it will be within their capabilities to attempt several of the friendly behaviours at once but for many students it is preferable to concentrate on one skill at a time. Rather in the same way as a traditional small steps programme, the class might address a new friendly behaviour each day or each week, reviewing their progress regularly at the end of each day. Teachers and classes familiar with role plays might wish to introduce each new skill in this way so that there are many examples around prior to the children trying to use them.

Pupil skill: friendship skills

For children who have previously been unable to maintain positive relationships or keep friends, a written record of the friendly things that happen is tangible proof that they are indeed able to be friends. The friendship audit carried out over the period of a week should not be done until all pupils have had the opportunity to see and try out friendship skills in action. (Figure 9.9)

There are alternative ways in which the sheet may be used. The best way to start is to target a few relationships only for each pupil. Those who have had problems forming relationships are not likely to be able to relate easily to many others at first.

Divide the children into random groups of five. They then write the names of the four other pupils in their group onto the back of the audit. Each child's name should be written in a different colour. They also need to decide the other two skills that their group think are friendly that they want to record. As the week progresses they each chart the number of friendly deeds they do for each other, using coloured ticks to represent each child in their group. This encourages group support for a child who still finds maintaining friendships difficult. It is in the interest of all the group to help that person to be friendly while it is also in that group's co-operative interest to be friendly towards that person. In addition the group structure for the audit helps form new relationships between children who would not ever have become friends without the task. Finally, it makes clear to children that they can behave in a friendly way towards each other even when they are not best friends.

Another way to use the audit is for pupils to record all friendly behaviours towards them by any other pupil. This can mean for a class of thirty that there are going to be (hopefully) many, many ticks very quickly. If your regime has been successful the children should spend all their time recording their friendly responses. If this worries you then regard the exercise as Maths, data handling!

The audit is very useful in helping pupils maintain their new skills by periodically asking them to audit the friendly behaviours that they receive. Change the random groups to encourage as many new relationships as possible.

Making the link between friendly deeds, relationships and positive feelings of worth

As we have stressed, the disruptive behaviour many children in school display is due to damage to their self-esteem. This damage can be so severe that helping them to attribute academic and social success to themselves and so raising their self-esteem can be very difficult. In our experience these pupils need to constantly hear good things about themselves from as many sources as possible. The sources within the control of the teacher are the teaching staff, the peer group, and to a lesser extent the ancillary staff in school. The parents can be influenced too, especially if the teacher spends time in forming positive relationships with them, and tells them about the improved behaviour that the child is showing. On this occasion overstating the positive can be very beneficial, and giving precise, detailed information of a positive nature can help tremendously. Many, but not all, of these parents are also suffering from a low

Friendly Behaviour Audit

Date: From .... to ....   Name:......................................

	Choosing to spend time with me	Helping me with my work	Sharing with me	- - - - - - - - - - -	- - - - - - - - - - - -
Monday					
Tuesday					
Wednesday					
Thursday					
Friday					
Saturday					
Sunday					

Choose other examples of friendly behaviour and write them in the chart.
Put a tick in a box each time someone does something friendly to you.
Change the number of friendly things you do to others.
Try doing this audit again in later in the term. Have people got more friendly towards you ?

Figure 9.9   Friendly behaviour audit

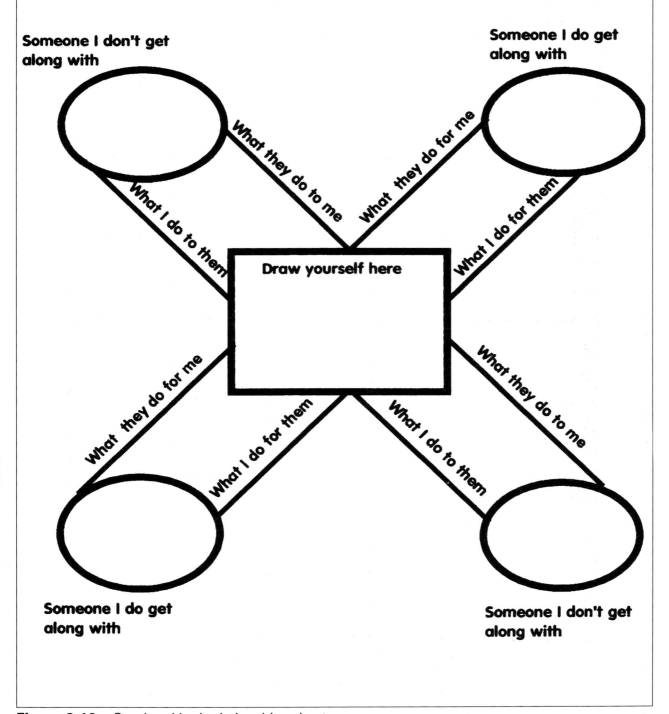

Good and Bad Relationships: What do we do?

Think about the pupils in your class. In the oval shapes, draw two who you get along with and two you don't. Draw yourself in the centre. Think about one thing that you do to or for them and one thing they do to or for you. Write these along the lines.

Figure 9.10 Good and bad relationships sheet

129

self-esteem and the 'telling off' by the teacher because of their son or daughter's behaviour might actually be taken out on the child later by verbal or even physical means.

It is important for children, after being given this praise for their efforts in behaviour and relationships, to be given the opportunity to reflect on the difference that their behaviour is making to the way they feel. If this is not given some attention then the child might continue to attribute their new found relationships to the skills of others. They might believe that they have friends now because the teacher is good at their job or is nice to them. They might think that their friends are friendly just because they are practising the skills. All of these might be true, but what pupils with problems in relationships often seem to lack is the ability to see that the fact that they are behaving in a friendly way too has made people respond to them, and like them for themselves. The Good and Bad Relationships Sheet (figure 9.10) is just one way of helping all the children make the links between their own behaviour towards others and the reciprocal nature of that behaviour. If they are nice to others then it is more likely that others will be nice back. Some, if not all, children need to be helped in understanding that it is not them that people did not like but what they did, and this is what they have the power to alter. My Helpful Tree is another way of allowing children to see the connection between their own behaviour and others' feelings towards them, (figure 9.11).

Peer tutoring as a structured friendship

When training peer tutors to help younger children, we noticed that many of the skills we were encouraging were not just teaching skills, such as how long to allow a pause and when to help out with a word, but friendship skills such as praising and complimenting, listening and helping, sharing and spending time together. Peer tutoring seemed to be a structured form of friendship where, although the curriculum was the basis for the meeting, social skills were modelled in a way very helpful to children with emotional and behavioural difficulties. It is because of this we have devoted a small section of this chapter to this area of supportive work.

Within the scope of this book a full assessment of the success of peer tutoring cannot be given. Those interested in this aspect might wish to refer to *The Peer Tutoring Handbook* by Keith Topping (1988). However, we wish to mention it here because of its potential in both helping overcome the learning difficulties which we believe are often caused by the emotionally negative situation the child finds him/herself in at school, and adding yet another positive relationship as a model for the child. Positive academic and social feedback can be given very effectively by the peer tutor, who in the role of teacher can have a great effect upon the process of enhancing self-esteem.

What we would recommend however, is that the peer tutoring is set up across as wide a group of students as possible, not just those who have learning difficulties. Bright children who feel excluded from this opportunity to be in a structured supportive friendship with a child from outside their normal peer group might feel rejected. This was indeed the case for a girl, who being a successful reader had not been included in the Web Club, a peer tutored reading scheme in her school. So successful had this been in allowing the

Figure 9.11   Helpful tree

children with difficulties to feel chosen and special that she felt left out! What she reported was missing the chance to have a special friend in the older class.

Although books on peer tutoring have their main focus on reading, peer tutoring need not be confined to reading skills. The use of the pupil group to help each other can be very effective in a wide variety of situations. For mixed age and ability classes it can provide teachers with potentially thirty ancillary helpers in each class.

The use of same-age mixed ability pairs can give students the same effects as cross-age tutoring. Similar ability pairing on shared research can be effective when the difficulty is behavioural rather than in learning. The common aim is to find out something but working with a 'friend' can help both students to know each other better, encourage them to use their communication skills, and allow relationships to develop further. As stated earlier, the pupils will need to be specifically taught friendship skills if this is to be a positive experience or it may prove to be destructive. Indeed, many teachers would say, 'He can't work with anyone, they'll only argue'. That might be true, if they have not been taught how not to argue!

The key element of this approach seems to be not the type of activity being taught, for example reading, maths, art, sport; or the age group or relative skills of the tutors or tutees, but the fact that the students are given total responsibility for the tutoring. It is this responsibility that allows them to attribute the success they experience to their own efforts and not regard it as something that happened because of another person. It might not be just the tutoring that ensures success. The feeling of being responsible can be enhanced very easily by entrusting the child to go to fetch their tutee without teacher supervision, by giving the children the task of designing a work sheet or game that will help to teach a particular skill or concept, or by asking them to choose and prepare a story book prior to working with the child.

On one occasion a pupil who had failed to read well, and so was very poorly motivated by even the more 'interesting' activities, worked for hours to produce materials to help him to teach an infant reading skills. The skills he was teaching were in fact the skills he himself had failed to acquire but this seemed to present no barrier when he was asked to overcome the difficulties for another child. The resulting change in attitude and improved skills was dramatic.

Why is Peer Tutoring effective for pupils with emotional and behavioural difficulties?

We, and the teachers with whom we work, have found that both being tutored by a peer and being a peer tutor can have dramatic effects on pupils with difficulties. There are many reasons why this might be so. It is probable that it is the interaction between all these factors which make peer tutoring worth great consideration as a classroom structure:

- Children with emotional and behavioural difficulties may have had a conflict with authority figures, especially in the school environment. A well trained peer tutor can sometimes more easily find a way through their defences. There is less of a power struggle and so it is easier for that pupil not to push against the structures imposed by the peer tutoring system.

- Peer tutoring also takes place on a one-to-one basis, with no audience to heighten any feelings of failure; mistakes can be made in relative safety. This is surely what teachers often find when they get difficult children alone on a one-to-one basis. It may be the reason why so many teachers feel the need for adult support to allow that child to be in a small group or in a one-to-one situation with an adult.

- A peer tutor can sometime express a concept and 'get through' because they are only a few steps ahead themselves. They find it easier to find and use the simple language necessary to provide certain ideas. Basically, they can talk in the language the pupil understands, particularly if they, unlike many teachers, share the same cultural and social background.

- The teacher benefits because the highly emotional nature of the relationship with a difficult child is taken off their hands for a short time.
- The benefit to the child being tutored is raised levels of on-task behaviour, raised experience of praise, raised success, raised feedback levels and raised self-esteem.
- For pupils with emotional problems being a tutor has immense benefits. For all children, being in the role of tutor has been shown (Topping, 1988) to raise their skills and their levels of self-esteem even more than those of pupils being tutored. This effect clearly can be of benefit to those with emotional and behavioural problems.
- Behaviours can also be influenced by being a peer tutor. The most violent of pupils, when asked to teach in the nursery and help the smallest children with their 'pretend' play, showed great skill and patience. He was, as the teacher reported, 'as gentle as a lamb'.
- Disruptive pupils can become locked into their role by the expectations of the group and their peers. Work through peer tutoring can begin to break this hold on these students and they can begin to try out a new role.
- Giving children responsibility is also an important factor in the success of peer tutoring for pupils with emotional and behavioural difficulties.

A role of responsibility

When teachers are talking about those pupils with behavioural difficulties in their class, the last thing they might feel like doing is handing them some responsibility as they seen unable even to be responsible for their own actions. However, being treated as responsible, in the same way as negative teacher expectations can have a negative effect, increases the amount of responsibility shown. Peer tutoring is one way in which we suggest small measures of responsibility can be given, but pupils will need to be seen in a responsible role by their peer group as well if their changed behaviour is to remain.

There are cases where pupils who are disruptive because they want to be first in everything, usually through a sense of insecurity about their own worth, can be helped by being put in charge of a group of their peers.

A child who needed to shout others down when in a small group, was destroying the whole group activity. This group were trying to plan a contribution to a class assembly and were being prevented from doing so by the child who wanted everyone to listen to him, he wanted every part in the action and was unprepared to listen to anyone else. He was becoming more and more aggressive and the group more and more frustrated.

This child was made the film director and cameraman. Using a video camera (although this may also be done with an imaginary camera to the same effect) he was legitimately able to tell the others what to do. He was allowed to demonstrate how he wanted it done but what he could not do was to try to take over and do it all himself as he had also to operate the camera. The resulting film was then to become part of the assembly presentation.

He was given responsibility for the success of the film as director, but the peer group was still there to add their own skills and their efforts in order to make

133

the project a success. The importance of responsibility was clear when another group, with an adult ancillary involved, made a good film but clearly made no progress in terms of changed behaviour.

Taking responsibility is not just reserved for inside the classroom or the curriculum. Helping with dinner time serving, supervising playground areas, monitoring storage areas of school equipment or putting out of equipment prior to lessons are all easy to organise and effective in producing changes in behaviour. Examples of certificates are given in this book that celebrate responsible behaviour in non-academic settings and are ways of publicly showing that the pupil can and should be seen in a 'new role'.

A new role in the peer group

Disruptive pupils, as we have described, can carry the negative feelings of a class group or be 'scapegoated' for crimes that the others wish they dare commit.

As clearly argued earlier, one of the difficulties encountered by teachers of children with behavioural problems is that their disruption is such that their relationships with their peers and with the teacher are increasingly negative. They just 'cannot get on' with other children. Activities that the teacher finds disruptive earn negative feedback from the teacher. The pupil then begins to behave in an increasingly negative way, self-fulfilling the prophecy. The teacher might fall into the trap of low expectations and have a readiness to blame that child for misdemeanours that are not in fact attributable to them. Peer tutoring is just one of the ways by which such children, who are locked into that 'blamed' role can move out.

As the peer group begin to see one pupil in the negative role then they too begin to attribute other 'crimes' to that person. These might not even be related to the initial behavioural problem that the child has exhibited. A recent example was when there was an incident in a classroom where a child's lunch box was stolen. Mark was a very intelligent and articulate boy who was

Figure 9.12　A new role for the peer group

disruptive through talking out of turn. Over a period he had developed more and more disruptive behaviours, many stemming from his desire to impress the other children whilst lacking the social skills to become their friend. He had become the 'bad boy' of the class. When the lunch box was stolen the news quickly spread that Mark had stolen it, even though Mark had never stolen anything else to their knowledge. The children in the class assured the teacher that they had seen Mark taking it, they had seen Mark eating its contents, there were eye witnesses. This was a clear case of scapegoating, where someone with negative aspects in their behaviour was assumed to have all negative traits, even though this was blatantly not true. Mark was in fact not guilty of the crime, the children having failed to realise that Mark was indeed absent from school that morning.

Children who are thus awarded all the negative feelings of a group find it difficult to break out of that negative role and change their patterns of behaviour. They begin to believe that as everyone thinks that they are bad they might as well be bad. If this badness is particularly linked with the school and classroom environment then the child will very soon experience all school as bad and again live down to their reputation. They become more and more entrenched in their role as the 'bad one', trying out more and more behaviours which receive negative feedback, thus assuring them that they are indeed as bad as everyone thought.

For these children, enabling them to experience school life in a different role is essential if they are to be enabled to change their behaviour. It is no use waiting for them to change so that they can be rewarded for it is very unlikely to happen, so fixed are they in their bad behaviour role. For teachers it is very helpful to regard the behaviour as the acting out of a role in a drama. They can then set about rewriting the drama, and attributing new roles to such difficult and disruptive pupils. Sometimes this can be very difficult as the child will not willingly give up their part, they have learnt the script and they are confident in their performance. The teacher as class director has however the power to give out different parts in the drama.

Powerful effects have been achieved by reversing the negative role of disruptive children. Making the bully the protector, giving the child with learning difficulties the role of tutor, giving the victim the role of group leader, giving the child who shouts charge of children who are unwell, may all seem unlikely but have all proved to be effective in allowing both the child themselves and the peer group the chance to see that the person is more than their role, and can be different in different circumstances. It gives them a chance.

Rewarding and celebrating new skills

The skills we are referring to here are not academic skills but new behaviours. There are rewards and praise aplenty for academic success but schools and teachers need to reward good behaviour with their praise. In the earlier chapters in this book we noted that poor behaviour was most often reprimanded whilst good behaviour was rarely given equivalent praise. Systems of reward and praise should be, in our view, as public as the 'telling off' that so many of these children have endured. If a child has been sent out of assembly for wriggling, then the awarding of praise, either verbal or tangible in a certificate will redress this imbalance. Some such certificates are shown throughout this book. These designs can easily be supplemented by changing the name of the positive behaviour in the title box. There is evidence from our own experience and from Records of Achievement, with their emphasis on publicly celebrating all pupils' successes, that not only do children treasure these awards but they also affect the feelings of self worth, and are also helpful in raising the self-esteem of parents who are shown them.

Conclusion

Damaged pupils try to damage others, the pain and frustration that teachers often feel is the pain and frustration of the pupils. The reason we have written this book is that it is our experience and therefore our belief that teachers can not only minimise the damage that has been done to children and youngsters, 'out there', but they can also make a profound difference. Not only do schools make a difference, teachers make a difference. If children can have access to teachers who help them to become confident and secure beings, who deep inside themselves know that they are worthwhile, then they can start to deal constructively with the other adults in their lives who may be unpredictable, inconsistent and unable to give much positive feedback because of their own childhood experiences. It is possible to give pupils the skills to learn that when adults are unreasonable it is not their fault. It is possible to teach even quite young reception children the skills to be able to offer comfort and support to the one who in the sharing circle declares that he thinks that his step daddy doesn't like toys, because his step daddy threw away all his toys.

Despite social class, ethnic group and gender difficulties and expectations, despite the incredible poverty that many of our children endure, we can help to make them strong.

As the five year old son of one of the authors said the other day, 'We do comforting *and* fighting in our gang mummy.' When he was asked whose idea that was, he said it was his – some of the training is working.

BIBLIOGRAPHY

Abercrombie, M.L.J. (1978) *Talking to Learn*, Guilford Surrey: Society for Research into Higher Education.

Adler, A. (1927) *The Practice and Theory of Individual Psychology*, New York: Harcourt, Brace & Co.

Adler, A. (1930) *The Education of Children*, Chicago: Gateway.

Alexander, R., Rose, J., Woodhead, C. (1992) *Curriculum Organisation and Classroom Practice in Primary Schools: a discussion paper*, The 'Three Wise Men' report, London: D.E.S.

Allport, G. (1950) *The Nature of Personality*, Reading, Mass.: Addison-Wesley Press.

Audit Commission and HMI, (1992) *Getting in on the Act, Provision for Pupils with Special Education Needs*, London: H.M.S.O..

Balson, M. (1982) *Understanding Classroom Behaviour*, Victoria: Australian Council for Educational Research.

Bandura, A. (1969) *Principles of Behaviour Modification*, New York: Holt, Rinehart and Winston.

Bandura, A. (1977) *Social Learning Theory*, Englewood Cliffs, NJ: Prentice-Hall.

Barnes, D. (1976) *From Communication to Curriculum*, Harmondsworth: Penguin.

Berne, E. (1964) *Games People Play: The Psychology of Human Relations*, New York: Grove Press.

Bernstein, B. (1972) *Class Codes and Control Volume 2*, London: Routledge and Kegan Paul.

Bolton, R. (1979) *People Skills*, New York: Spectrum/Prentice Hall.

Borba, M. and Borba, C. (1978) *Self-Esteem A Classroom Affair, 101 Ways to Help Children Like Themselves*, San Francisco: Harper and Row.

Brookover, W.B., Paterson, A., and Thomas, S. (1962) *Self-Concept of Ability and School Achievement: 1.*, E. Lansing, Mich.: Educational Publishing Services.

Brookover, W.B., LePere, J.M. Hamachek, D., Thomas, S., and Erikson, E.L. (1965) *Self-Concept of Ability and School Achievement: 11.*, E. Lansing, Mich.: Educational Publishing Services.

Brookover, W.B., Erikson, E.L., and Joiner, L.M. (1967) *Self-Concept of Ability and School Achievement: 111.*, E. Lansing, Mich.: Educational Publishing Services.

Burns, R,B. (1982) *Self-Concept Development and Education*, London: Holt,

Rinehart and Winston.

Canfield, J. and Wells, H.C. (1976) *100 Ways to Enhance Self-Concept in the Classroom*, Mass: Allyn and Bacon.

Canter, L. and Canter, M. (1976) *Assertive Discipline: A Take-Charge Approach for Today's Educator*, Seal Beach, California: Canter and Associates.

Charlton, T. and David, K. (1989) *Managing Misbehaviour: Strategies for Effective Management of Behaviour in Schools*, Basingstoke: Macmillan.

Chessum, R. (1980) 'Teachers' ideologies and pupil disaffection, in Barton, L., Meighan, R. and Walker, S. (eds), *Schooling, Ideology and the Curriculum*, Lewes: Falmer Press.

Cohen, L. and Cohen, A. (1987) *Disruptive Behaviour, A source book for Teachers*, London: Harper Row.

Coopersmith, S. (1967) *Antecedants of Self-Esteem*, San Francisco: W.H. Freeman and Co.

Cooper, P., Smith, C.J., Upton, G. (1994) *Emotional Behaviour Difficulties, Theory to Practice*, London: Routledge.

Cronk, K. (1987) *Teacher-Pupil Conflict in Secondary Schools*, Lewes: Falmer Press.

Dreikurs, R. (1968) *Psychology in the Classroom: A Manual for Teachers*, New York: Harper Row.

D.E.S. (1989) *Discipline in Schools: Report of the Committee of Enquiry chaired by Lord Elton*, 'The Elton Report', London: H.M.S.O..

D.F.E. (1993) *Education Act 1993*, London H.M.S.O.

D.F.E. (1994) *Code of Practice for Special Educational Needs*, London: D.F.E.

D.F.E. (1994) *Pupils with Problems*, London: D.F.E.

Egan, G. (1975) *The Skilled Helper*, Monterey, California: Brookes Cole.

Fish, J. (1985) *Special Education: The Way Ahead*, Milton Keynes: Open University Press.

Flanders, N. (1970) *Analysing Teacher Behaviour*, Reading, Mass: Addison-Wesley Press.

Fontana, D. (1985) *Classroom Control: Understanding and Guiding Classroom Behaviour*, London: Methuen/British Psychological Society.

Fontana, D. (1992) *Psychology For Teachers*, second edition, Basingstoke: British Psychological Society with Macmillan Press Ltd.

Furlong, V.J. (1984) 'Black resistance in the liberal comprehensive' in Delamont, S. (eds). *Explorations in Classroom Observation*, Chichester: Wiley

Fuller, M. (1982) 'Young, female and black,' in Cashmore, R. and Troyna, B. (Eds) *Black Youth in Crisis*, London: George Allen and Unwin.

Galloway, D., Ball, T., Bloomfield, D. and Seyd, R. (1982), *Schools and Disruptive Pupils*, London: Longman.

Galloway, D. (1985) *Schools, Pupils and Special Educational Need*, London: Croom Helm.

Galloway, D. (1987), 'Teachers, parents and other professionals', in K. David, and T. Charlton (Eds) *The Caring Role of the Primary School*, London: Macmillan.

Galloway, D. and Goodwin, C. (1979) *The Education of Slow Learning and Maladjusted Children*, London: Longman.

Galloway, D. and Goodwin, C.(1987) *The Education of Disturbing Children: Pupils with Learning and Adjustment Problems*, Harlow: Longman.

Galton, M., Simon, B. and Croll, P. (1980) *Inside The Primary Classroom*, London: Routledge and Kegan Paul.

Gordan, T. (1974) *TET: Teacher Effectiveness Training*, New York: David McKay.

Great Britain (1993) Parliament, House of Commons Education (Schools) Act 1993, chapter 35, London, H.M.S.O.

Hall, E. and Hall, C. (1988) *Human Relations in Education*, London: Routledge.

Hall, E. and Hall, C. and Leech, A. (1990) *Scripted Fantasy in the Classroom*, London: Routledge.

Hamachek, D. (1987) *Encounters with the Self*, New York: Holt Rinehart and Winston.

Hamblin, D. (1974) *The Teacher and Counselling*, Oxford: Blackwell.

Hamblin, D. (1989) *Staff Development for Pastoral Care*, Oxford: Blackwell.

Hargreaves, D.H. (1967) *Social Relations in a Secondary School*, London: Routledge and Kegan Paul.

Hargreaves, D.H., Hester, S.K. and Mellor, F.J. (1975) *Deviance in Classrooms*, London: Routledge and Kegan Paul.

Hargreaves, D.H. (1982) *The Challenge of the Comprehensive School*, London: Routledge and Kegan Paul.

Hargreaves, D.H. and Hopkins, D. (1991) *The Empowered School: the management and practice of development and planning*, London: Cassell.

HMI (1977) *Ten Good Schools*, London: H.M.S.O.

HMI (1979) *Aspects of Secondary Education*, London: H.M.S.O.

HMI (1988) *The Curriculum from 5–16*; the responses to Curriculum Matters 2, D.E.S., H.M.I., London: H.M.S.O.

Holt, J. (1964) *How Children Fail*, Harmondsworth: Penguin.

ILEA (1984) *Improving Secondary Schools*, (The Hargreaves Report), London: ILEA.

ILEA. (1985) *Educational Opportunities For All?* Report of the Committee Reviewing Provision to meet Special Educational Needs, (The Fish Report), London: ILEA.

ILEA (1990) *Explusions and Exclusions from Schools*, London: ILEA.

James, W. and Jongeward, D. (1971) *Born To Win*, New York: Signet, Addison Wesley Publishing Company.

James, W. (1890) *Principles of Psychology*, Vol. 1, New York: Henry Holt.

Johnson, D.W. and Johnson, F.P. (1987) *Joining Together: Group Theory and Group Skills*, (3rd edition), New York: Prentice-Hall International.

Jones, V.F. and Jones, L.S. (1990) *Comprehensive Classroom Management, Motivating and Managing Students*, (3rd Edition), Boston: Allyn and Bacon.

Jourard, S. (1971) *The Transparent Self*, New York: Van Nostrand Reinhold.

Kirkpatrick S.W. and Sanders, D.M. (1978) 'Body Image Stereotypes: A

Developmental Comparison', *Journal of Genetic Psychology*, 126, pp, 169–176.
Kirchner, P. and Vondraek, S. (1975), 'Perceived Sources of Esteem in Early Childhood', *Journal of Genetic Psychology* 126, pp 169–176.

Lawrence, D. (1987) *Enhancing Self Esteem in the Classroom*, London: Paul Chapman Publishing.
Lawson, M. (1980)'Development of Body Build Stereotypes, Peer Ratings and Self-Esteem in Australian Children, *Journal of Psychology*, 104, p. 111–118.
Lewis, A.R. (1971) 'The Self Concept of Adolescent ESN Boys,' *British Journal of Educational Psychology*, 41, pp. 222–223.
Lund, R. (1987) 'The Self-Esteem of Children with Emotional and Behavioural Difficulties', *Maladjustment and Therapeutic Education*, 5, No.1.

Maslow, A.H. (1954) *Motivation and Personality*, Harper and Row.
Maslow, A.H. (1962) *Towards a Psychology of Being*, London: Nostrand.
McNamara, S. and Moreton, G. (1993) *Teaching Special Needs*, London: David Fulton Publishers.
McNamara, S. (1994) 'Counselling Skills in the Classroom' in Harrison, J. and Edwards, J., *Developing Health Education in the Curriculum*, London: David Fulton Publishers.
Mercer, N. (1991), 'Learning Through Talk', Article 1.2 in *Talk for Learning 5–16* an in-service pack on Oracy for Teachers, Milton Keynes: Open University.
Merrick, N. and Manuel, G. (1991) 'Authorities want end to exclusion loophole', *Times Educational Supplement*, 25 October.
Mortimore, P. Sammons, L. Stoll, L. Ecob, R. (1988) *School Matters*, London: Open Books.
Munro, E.A., Mantrei, R.J. and Small, J.J. (1979), *Counselling, a Skills Approach*, London: Methuen.
Myers, K. (1987) *Genderwatch*, London: SCDC Publishers.

Norman, K. (1991) *Teaching Talking and Learning in Key Stage One*, NCC and National Oracy Project.

Purkey, W. (1970) *Self-Concept and School Achievement*, New York: Prentice Hall.
Pyke, N. (1991) 'Alarm over sharp rise in exclusions', *Times Educational Supplement*, 4, October.

Reid, K., Hopkins, D. and Holly, P. (1987) *Towards the Effective School*, Oxford: Blackwell.
Reynolds, D. (1976) 'The Delinquent School', in Hammersely, M. and Woods, P. (Eds) *The Process of Schooling*, Milton Keynes: Open University Press.
Reynolds, D. (1984) 'The school for vandals, a sociological portrait of the disaffection prone school', in Frude, N. and Gault, H. (Eds), *Disruptive Behaviour in Schools*, Chichester: Wiley.
Reynolds, D. (1985) *Studying School Effectiveness*, Lewes: Falmer Press.
Rogers, C. (1951) *Client Centred Therapy*, Boston: Houghton Mifflin.
Rogers, C. (1961) *On Becoming a Person: A Therapist's View of Psychotherapy*, Boston: Houghton Mifflin.

Rogers, C. (1967) *Person to Person*, London: Souvenir Press.

Rogers, C. (1969) *Freedom to Learn*, Colombus: Merrill.

Rogers, C. (1983) *Freedom to Learn for the 80's*, Columbus: Merrill.

Rosenthal, R. and Jacobsen, L. (1968) *Pygmalion in the Classroom*, New York: Holt, Rinehart and Winston.

Rutter, M. (1975) *Helping Troubled Children*, Harmondsworth: Penguin.

Rutter, M., Maughan, B., Mortimore, P. and Ouston, J. (1979) *Fifteen Thousand Hours*, London: Open Books.

Seligman, M.E.P. (1975) *Helplessness: On Depression, Development and Death*, San Francisco: Freeman.

Sheldon, B. (1982) *Behaviour Modification*, Tavistock Library of Social Work Practice.

Skinner, B.F. (1968) *The Technology of Teaching*, New York: Appleton-Century-Crofts.

Skinner, B.F. (1974) *About Behaviourism*, London: Jonathan Cape.

Spender, D. (1982) *Invisible Women: The Schooling Scandal*, London: Women's Press.

Sullivan, H.S. (1953) *Interpersonal Theory of Psychiatry*, New York: Norton.

Tann, S. (1988) *Developing Language in the Primary Classroom*, London: Cassell.

Tattum, D. (1982) *Disruptive Pupils in Schools and Units*, Chichester: Wiley.

Tattum, D. (1986) *Management of Disruptive Pupil Behaviour in Schools*, Chichester: Wiley.

Tattum, D. (1989) *Bullying in Schools*, Stoke on Trent: Trentham Books.

Thompson, J.L. (1986) *All Right for Some: the Problem of Sexism,* London: Hutchinson.

Tomlinson, S., Taylor, M.J., and Hegarty, S. (1987) 'Ethnic Minority Children in Special Education,' in Cohen L. and Cohen A. *Disruptive Behaviour, A Sourcebook for Teachers.*

Topping, K. (1988) *The Peer Tutoring Handbook: Promoting co-operative Learning*, Beckenham: Croom Helm.

Tough, J. (1976) *Listening to Children Talking*, A guide to the appraisal of children's use of language, Communication Skills in Early Childhood Project, London: Ward Locke in association with Drake Educational Associates.

Tough, J. (1977) *Development of Meaning*, London: Allen and Unwin Educational Books.

Train, A. (1993) *Helping the Aggressive Child, How to deal with Difficult Children*, London Souvenir Press.

Underwood Committee (1955) *Report of the Committee on Maladjusted Children.* London: H.M.S.O.

Vygotsky, L.S. (1962) *Thought and Learning*, New York: Wiley.

Vygotsky, L.S. (1978) *Mind in Society*, London: Harvard University Press.

Weiner, G. (1985) *Just a Bunch of Girls: Feminist approaches to Schooling,* Oxford: O.U.P.

Wells, G. (1986) *The Meaning Makers: Children Learning Language and Using*

Language to Learn, London: Hodder and Stoughton.

Westmacott, E.V.S. and Cameron, R.J. (1981) *Behaviour can Change*, London and Basingstoke: Macmillan Educational.

Wheldall, K. (ed.) (1987) *The Behaviourist in the Classroom*, London: Allen and Unwin.

Wheldall, K. (ed.) (1992) *Discipline in Schools: Psychological Perspectives on the Elton Report*, London: Routledge.

Wheldall, K. and Merrett, F. (1984) *Positive Teaching: The Behavioural Approach*, London: Allen and Unwin.

Wheldall, K. and Merrett, F. (1992) 'Effective classroom behaviour management: positive teaching', in Wheldall, K. (Ed) *Discipline in Schools: Psychological Perspectives on the Elton Report*, London: Routledge.

Wheldall, K. and Glynn, T. (1989) *Effective Classroom Learning: A Behavioural Interactionist Approach to Teaching*, London: Basil Blackwell.

Wilkinson, A. (1965) 'Spoken English', *Educational Review*, Occasional Publication. No. 2, University of Birmingham.

Wills, D. (1960) *Throw Away Thy Rod*, London: Victor Gollancz.

Willis, P. (1977) *Learning to Labour: how working class kids get working class jobs*, Farnborough: Saxon House.

Woods, P. (1990) *Teacher Skills and Strategies*, Lewes: Falmer Press.

Index

PE 87